ISBN 978-0-266-94993-0
PIBN 10914396

This book is a reproduction of an important historical work. Forgotten Books uses
state-of-the-art technology to digitally reconstruct the work, preserving the original format
whilst repairing imperfections present in the aged copy. In rare cases, an imperfection in
the original, such as a blemish or missing page, may be replicated in our edition. We do,
however, repair the vast majority of imperfections successfully; any imperfections that
remain are intentionally left to preserve the state of such historical works.

THE

PRACTICAL

SPELLING-BOOK,

WITH

READING LESSONS.

BY T. H. GALLAUDET,
AND
HORACE HOOKER.

HARTFORD:
WM. JAS. HAMERSLEY.
1856.

Stereotyped by
RICHARD H. HOBBS,
Hartford, Conn.

PREFACE.

THE prominent features of this work, together with the labor expended upon it, will appear from a simple statement of the manner in which the authors proceeded in its preparation. Taking a Dictionary containing between forty and fifty thousand words, they carefully examined each, to ascertain whether it was in common use, and simple in its orthography. If it was found to be so, it was put down in the class of easy words. If it contained any difficulty deserving notice, the inquiry was made in what this consisted. These difficulties were classified as they occurred, and the words arranged accordingly. The few words which could not be thus classed, were placed by themselves. The result was one great division of the words into the comparatively easy and hard, and the subdivision of the latter into their respective classes. The easy were arranged in lessons in the first part of the book, to prepare the way for the more difficult. This slow, inductive process led to the notice of some peculiar facts respecting the spelling of certain classes of words, which will be found in the questions appended to the lessons,—and which, it is thought, will furnish considerable aid in this very perplexing part of education.

In thus attempting to cope with the many and singular anomalies in the orthography of our language, it has not been made a leading principle of classification to have the lessons composed of words of the same number of syllables, accented on the same syllable. Nor can this be done, if it is the true object of a Spelling-Book to meet the *greatest* difficulties in orthography,—which are found in words variously accented, and differing in the number of syllables. For example, in words that end in *ant* and *ent*, as *tenant*, *prudent*; in *ar* and *er*, as *pillar*, *banner*; and in numerous similar cases, the perplexity usually lies in its being difficult, on account of the obscure pronunciation of the unaccented syllables, to detect, *by the ear merely*, the proper letters to be used. In other words,—and our language abounds in them,— such as, *boat, note*; *through, new*; *humane, remain*; and similar ones, it arises from the same sounds being represented by different vowels, or combinations of vowels. It is evident, therefore, that in both these cases, the classification of words according to accent and the number of syllables should hold a subordinate place. Still, in this work, the accentuation of every word is effectually provided for.

A few words containing more than one considerable difficulty, have been placed, on that account, in two lessons. A few, also, concerning the orthography of which good writers still differ, have been inserted in two forms; leaving it for the teacher to give a preference if he pleases. Provision has also been made, in some cases, for diversity of pronunciation of nearly equal authority.

The omission of obsolete, and for the most part, of technical words ; of such as may be derived from primitives without any danger of mistake in the spelling ; of easy compounds ; and of others formed by the addition of the common prefixes and suffixes, has afforded room for a very copious collection of those words which the great mass of the people are in the habit of using, or which occur in their reading.

The plan of classification, it is thought, will cultivate a methodical memory, and afford, in the various ways in which the lessons may be recited, peculiar advantages for keeping up the attention of the scholar, and for testing his accuracy.   It furnishes, also, in connection with the questions appended to the lessons, a practical analysis of the principal anomalies in orthography, and, by a thorough exercise in them, impresses them more deeply on the mind.   It has admitted the introduction of simple reading lessons in a very early part of the book, combining interest with moral instruction.   These lessons, at first, consist of words which the scholar has previously learned to spell.   Afterwards, as he makes progress, a few harder ones are introduced for the first time, and placed also at the head of the lessons, that they may receive particular attention.

While the work is particularly designed for the use of common schools, it is believed that its general plan, together with the index, will make it eminently useful to the advanced classes in Academies and higher Seminaries ; as their attention can thus be directed immediately to what is more intricate, passing over the comparatively easy words in the first part of the book, with which they are supposed to be already familiar.

That their work is free from all deficiency or error, the authors have not the presumption to claim ; and they will be thankful for any suggestions which may enable them, hereafter, to correct and improve it.

OF LETTERS AND THEIR SOUNDS.

In the English Alphabet there are *twenty-six* letters; consisting of vowels and consonants.

A *vowel* is a letter which can be fully sounded by itself.

The vowels are, *a, e, i, o, u*; and *w* and *y* when they do not begin a word or syllable. When *w* and *y* begin a word or syllable, they are consonants.

A *consonant* is a letter which cannot be fully sounded without the help of a vowel. The consonants are *b, c, d, f, g, h, j, k, l, m, n, p, q, r, s, t, v, x, z*; and sometimes *w* and *y*.

A *diphthong* is the union of *two* vowels in one syllable, uttered at the same time; as *oi* in toil, *ou* in ground.

A *triphthong* is the union of *three* vowels, uttered in like manner; as *iew* in view.

In a *proper* diphthong both the vowels are sounded.

In an *improper* diphthong only *one* of the vowels is sounded; as *ea* in neat, *oa* in boat.

OF THE VOWELS.

A has *five* sounds; as in *hate, hat, bar, ball, wad.*

E has *three* sounds; as in *here, pen, they.* It, also, has a peculiar sound, as in *her, jerk.*

I has *four* sounds; as in *mine, pin, fatigue, bird.*

O has *four* sounds; as in *globe, not, move, son.*

U has *three* sounds; as in *cube, nut, bush.*

Y, when a *vowel*, has *two* sounds; as in *type, hymn.*

W, when a *vowel*, sounds like *u*, as in *few.*

Oi and *oy* sound as in *point, boy; eu, ew, ieu*, and *iew*, as *u* in *cube.*

OF THE CONSONANTS.

B has only *one* sound, as in *web, bid.*

C has *two* principal sounds. Before *a, o*, and *u*, it is hard like *k*, as in *came, cob, cut.* Before *e, i*, and *y*, it is *soft* like *s*, as in *cell, cite*, and *cymbal.*

D has *one* principal sound, as in *did.* It sometimes sounds like *t*, at the end of words, as in *mixed.*

F has only *one* sound, except in *of*, where it sounds like *v.*

G has *two* sounds: one, as in *gate*, and the other as in *gem.*

H denotes a *strong breathing* before the utterance of the succeeding vowel; as in *hate*. It is silent after *r*, as in *rhyme*.

J has one sound, as in *jet*, except in *hallelujah*, where it sounds like *y*.

K has but *one* sound, as in *kite*. Before *n* it is always silent

L has but *one* sound, as in *let*.

M has but *one* sound, as in *man*.

N has *two* sounds; one *pure*, as in *pen;* the other like *ng*, as in *thank*, pronounced *thangk*. It is silent at the end of a syllable, when preceded by *l* or *m*, as in *kiln, hymn*.

P has but *one* sound, as in *top*.

Q sounds like *k*, and is always followed by *u* sounded like *w*, as in *quake*, except when *u* is silent.

R has a rough sound, as in *rage;* and a *smooth* one as in *card*.

S has *two* principal sounds; one, as in *sun;* the *other* like *z*, as in *was*.

T has one principal sound, as in *time*.

V has but *one* sound, as in *vale, hive*.

W, when a consonant, has but *one* sound, as in *web*. Before *r* it is always silent, as in *wrote*. Before h, *w* is usually pronounced as if following it, as in *whip*.

X has *two* sounds; like *ks*, as in *box*, and like *gs*, as in *exist*.

Y, when a consonant, has but *one* sound, as in *yoke*.

Z has *one* principal sound, as in *haze, zone*.

Ch has *three* sounds; as in *chime*, in *ache*, and in *chaise*.

Gh, beginning a word, as in *ghost*, sounds like *g* as in gate. In the middle, or at the end of a word, it is sometimes *silent*, as in *right, plough;* and sometimes has the sound of *f, k*, or *g*.

Ph is usually pronounced like *f*, as in *phrase*.

Th has *two* sounds; *one* as in *thin;* the *other* as in *the*.

Sc has the sound of *sk* before *a, o, u*, and *r;* and of *s* before *e, i*, and *y*.

OF WORDS,

And the Marks in this Book, which direct their Pronunciation.

A *monosyllable* is a word of *one* syllable.

A *dissyllable* is a word of *two* syllables.

A *trissyllable* is a word of *three* syllables.

A *polysyllable* is a word of *four* or *more* syllables.

Silent letters in this book are printed in Italics; as in gnat, lim*b*.

The long vowels are marked thus; hāte, hēre, mīne, glōbe, cūbe, rhȳme.

The short vowels are marked thus; hăt, pĕn, pĭn, nŏt, nŭt, hўmn.

The figure 1 over *a*, denotes the sound of *a*, as in bär.

The figure 2 denotes the sound of *u*, as in bush.

The figure 3 denotes the sound of *a*, as in bȧll.

The figure 4 denotes the sound of *a*, as in wȧd.

The figure 5 over *ı* denotes the sound of *u*; as in bïrd.

C, c, marked thus, Ç, ç, has the sound of *s*, as in çhaise. This mark is called a cedilla.

Ch without this mark sounds as in chime, porch, except in Lesson 206, where it has the sound of k.

The same mark under *s*, denotes that it sounds like *z*; as in roṣe.

A dot under the *t*, in ṭh, denotes that *th* sounds as in ṭhe, ṭhine.

Th without this dot, is sounded as in thin, thistle.

The accented syllables are marked thus ; la′ dy, be long′.

Where a mark is placed over a vowel, it denotes, also, that the vowels in the monosyllables, and in the accented syllables of the succeeding words, have the same sound until a different mark is used.

The mark for accent over any word, denotes that the succeeding words, having an equal number of syllables, are accented on the same syllable until it is placed over a different one.

The pronunciation of some words is given in a parenthesis connected with them ; as *one* (wŭn), and sometimes in a note.

When two or more words are connected together by a brace, it denotes that they are spelt differently by good writers.

In this work, unless otherwise designated, *ou* sounds as in *bound*; *ow* as in *cow*; *ai* and *ay*, accented, as *a* in *hate*; and *ea*, as *e* in *here*.

DIRECTIONS TO TEACHERS.

The teacher should be careful to explain the marks used in this book, and see that the scholar is familiar with them.

The words as far as Lesson 30, are arranged to be spelt *across* the page ; in that and all the subsequent lessons, they are arranged to be spelt in perpendicular columns. The teacher, in hearing the lessons, may occasionally vary this order to advantage.

To test the accuracy of the scholar, let the teacher often put out words from the different columns *indiscriminately*, especially in those lessons where peculiar difficulties are contrasted with each other. For example ; in Lesson 76, let him give out a word ending in *o* ; then, another in *ow* ; or in *oe* ; or in *eau* ; and so on, to any extent he may deem necessary. Thus, also, in Lesson 135, and the three following, give out words ending in *ant* and *ent* from the different columns indiscriminately.

Be careful in asking the questions at the end of the lessons, to see that they are thoroughly understood by the scholar. The questions on the more difficult lessons, may be deferred, if the teacher deems best, till a review of such lessons.

Question the more advanced scholars on the heads of the difficult lessons. For example; in Lesson 76, let the teacher ask, in how many ways is the sound of *o* as in globe, represented in this lesson. If the scholar answers correctly, he will say. by *o, oa, ow, ew, ough, eau, owe,* and *oe.*

In Lesson 100, ask what are the various terminations in this lesson. The answer should be, *et, it, ute, ait, oat, ot, ut,* and *at.*

Another useful mode of hearing the more advanced scholars review the difficult lessons, is to call upon them, in turn, to mention words illustrating the difficulties. For example, in Lesson 84, let the teacher say; "Give me a word with *a* in it sounding as in hate—another with *ea,* having the same sound—another with *ai*—and another with *ei.*

Where words of peculiar orthography in a lesson are few in number, let the advanced scholars be called upon to repeat them, or to write them from memory on the blackboard. . For example. in Lesson 108, let them tell what words end in *ad;* what, in *od;* and what, in *ud.*

Where new and difficult words occur in the *Reading Lessons,* they are placed at the head of the lesson. The teacher should see that the scholar is familiar with them before he proceeds to the reading lesson.

When words of similar pronunciation, but *differently spelt,* occur in the same lesson, the teacher should direct the scholar to find their various significations in the table beginning on page 147. The teacher, also, as he gives out these words, should be careful to mention their significations. As, for example, in Lesson 76, will be found the words *bow* and *beau; dough* and *doe.*

The Alphabet, it will be seen, is divided into sections of *four letters;* each section to be thoroughly learned before proceeding to the next. After thus learning the small letters, let the scholar proceed to the italic, the capital, and the double letters.

The teacher is particularly requested, as the scholar advances in the lessons, to make him thoroughly acquainted with *the rules for spelling* on page 160; giving, and requiring him to give, additional illustrations. See additional remarks, page 163.

THE ALPHABET.

a	b	c	d	A	q	r	s	t	Q
b	d	a	c	B	r	t	q	s	R
c	a	d	b	C	s	q	t	r	S
d	c	b	a	D	t	s	r	q	T
e	f	g	h	E	u	v	w	x	U
f	h	e	g	F	v	x	u	w	V
g	e	h	f	G	w	u	x	v	W
h	g	f	e	H	x	w	v	u	X
i	j	k	l	I	y	z	&		Y
j	l	i	k	J	z	&	y		Z
k	i	l	j	K	&	z	y		&
l	k	j	i	L					
m	n	o	p	M					
n	p	m	o	N					
o	m	p	n	O					
p	o	n	m	P					

Italic.

a	b	c	d	e	f
g	h	i	j	k	l
m	n	o	p	q	r
s	t	u	v	w	x
y	z	&			

Double Letters, and Diphthongs.

fi ff fl ffi ffl æ œ

LESSON I.

ba	be	bi	bo	bu	by
da	de	di	do	du	dy
fa	fe	fi	fo	fu	fy
ha	he	hi	ho	hu	hy

LESSON II.

sa	se	si	so	su	sy
	ce	ci			cy
la	le	li	lo	lu	ly
ma	me	mi	mo	mu	my

LESSON III.

ka	ke	ki	ko	ku	ky
ca			co	cu	
na	ne	ni	no	nu	ny
pa	pe	pi	po	pu	py

LESSON IV.

ja	je	ji	jo	ju	jy
	ge	gi			gy
ra	re	ri	ro	ru	ry
ta	te	ti	to	tu	ty

LESSON V.

ga		go	gu		
va	ve	vi	vo	vu	vy
wa	we	wi	wo	wu	wy
za	ze	zi	zo	zu	zy

LESSON VI.

qua	que	qui	quo		
ya	ye	yi	yo		
ca	ce	ci	co	cu	cy
ga	ge	gi	go	gu	gy

In ce, ci, cy, c sounds like s.   In ge, gi, gy, g usually like j.
In ca. co. cu. c sounds like k.   In ga, go, gu, g sounds as in gate.

LESSON VII.

bla	ble	bli	blo	blu	bly
cla	cle	cli	clo	clu	cly
fla	fle	fli	flo	flu	fly
gla	gle	gli	glo	glu	gly
pla	ple	pli	plo	plu	ply
sla	sle	sli	slo	slu	sly

LESSON VIII.

bra	bre	bri	bro	bru	bry
cra	cre	cri	cro	cru	cry
dra	dre	dri	dro	dru	dry
fra	fre	fri	fro	fru	fry
gra	gre	gri	gro	gru	gry
pra	pre	pri	pro	pru	pry
tra	tre	tri	tro	tru	try
wra	wre	wri	wro	wru	wry

LESSON IX.

ska	ske	ski	sko	sku	sky
sha	she	shi	sho	shu	shy
spa	spe	spi	spo	spu	spy
sta	ste	sti	sto	stu	sty
spla	sple	spli	splo	splu	sply
spra	spre	spri	spro	spru	spry
stra	stre	stri	stro	stru	stry
pha	phe	phi	pho	phu	phy

LESSON X.

ābe	ēbe	ībe	ōbe	ūbe
ade	ede	ide	ode	ude
ake	eke	ike	oke	uke
ame	eme	ime	ome	ume
ane	ene	ine	one	une
ate	ete	ite	ote	ute

LESSON XI.

bābe	hē	kīte	rōpe	mūle
plate	here	lime	home	tube
cage	me	fire	hole	tune
rake	we	pile	colt	flute
dale	she	hive	mole	plume
gave	ye	side	note	mute

LESSON XII.

ab	eb	ib	ob	ub
ac	ec	ic	oc	uc
ad	ed	id	od	ud
af	ef	if	of	uf
ag	eg	ig	og	ug
al	el	il	ol	ul
am	em	im	om	um

LESSON XIII.

an	en	in	on	un
ap	ep	ip	op	up
ar	er	ir	or	ur
as	es	is	os	us
at	et	it	ot	ut
av	ev	iv	ov	uv
ax	ex	ix	ox	ux
az	ez	iz	oz	uz

LESSON XIV.

băg	hĕn	hĭm	pŏd	sŭn
ham	bed	lip	hot	cub
man	peg	rib	top	nut
cap	web	tin	dog	bud
bad	net	pig	cob	sup
hat	hem	kid	yon	mug
sap	vex	hit	fox	hum
wax	pen	fix	lot	tub
yam	yes	yelk	yet	yelp

LESSON XV.

Words in which s sounds like z.

aş haş iş hiş

LESSON XVI.

James has a top.
His kite is at home
Jane has a bag.
He gave me a pen.
The fox is in his hole.

LESSON XVII.

Words in which a sounds as in bar.

bar	car	far	mar	tar
ark	bark·	dark	hark	lark
mark	park	shark	spark	stark
ask	task	cask	flask	mask
asp	clasp	gasp	grasp	rasp
art	cart	dart	part	tart
hard	bard	card	lard	yard

LESSON XVIII.

Words in which a sounds as in ball.

ball	call	fall	gall	mail
hall	pall	stall	small	squall
tall	wall	all	war	ward
warm	warn	warp	want	wart ·
wasp	swarm	sward	bald	scald

LESSON XIX.

Words in which a sounds as in wad.

wad	wan	wand	wash	swab
swamp	swan	swap	salt	halt
quart	squad	squash	squat	waş

LESSON XX.

The hen is in the yard.
The dog barks at the hen.
He is a small dog.
It is bad to vex the hen.
Call the dog here.
A man gave me the dog.
He was a tall man.

LESSON XXI.

Words in which o sounds as in son.

son	ton	won	done	month
come	some	dove	love	glove
shove	front	word	work	world

LESSON XXII.

Words in which o sounds as in move, and oo as in fool; both being the same sound.

move	to	lose	do	prove
fool	pool	tool	stool	spool
bloom	boom	doom	gloom	loom
boon	noon	spoon	moon	soon
loop	sloop	coop	droop	too

LESSON XXIII.

Words in which u sounds as in bush, and oo, o, and ou, as in book; being the same sound.

bush	push	put	puss	pull
bull	full	book	cook	hook
look	nook	shook	rook	brook
crook	took	wool	wood	good
hood	stood	hoop	foot	root
soot	wolf	would	could	should

LESSON XXIV.

Puss sits by the fire.
She is warm.
She loves to sit by the fire.
Come, let us go.
We should do the task.
We should pile up the wood.
It is good to work.

LESSON XXV.

Words containing oi and oy.

boil	broil	coil	coin	join
loin	hoist	moist	joint	point
oil	soil	spoil	toil	void
boy	coy	cloy	joy	toy

LESSON XXVI.

Words containing ou and ow.

bound	sound	round	ground	hound
found	mound	shout	pout	rout
stout	out	count	fount	mount
cloud	loud	proud	flour	oust
cow	how	now	owl	fowl
down	drown	frown	gown	crowd

LESSON XXVII.

Words containing au and aw.

daub	fraud	haul	caul	maul
fault	vault	cause	clause	pause
caw	daw	draw	flaw	haw
jaw	law	paw	raw	saw
maw	straw	thaw	claw	awl
crawl	scrawl	sprawl	bawl	shawl
brawn	dawn	fawn	lawn	pawn

LESSON XXVIII.

James and his Hoop.

This boy is James.
He drives a hoop.
The hoop is round.
Look how fast he runs.
He makes the hoop go fast.
Boys love to drive hoops.
It is a good play.

A good boy loves his books *too*.

LESSON XXIX.

tīme	tīne	vīle	wīle	wīfe
hīre	mīre	spīre	pōst	bōne
plăn	răn	răg	răp	răt
sad	shad	shag	sham	slab
slam	slap	snag	snap	span
stag	tan	tap	trap	van
vat	wag	jam	wit	bit
pit	sit	wig	trip	din
fin	sin	win	bin	kin
pin	sod	sot	gun	run
fun	spun	tun	sum	snug
jug	stub	mud	rut	shut

LESSON XXX.

Words of two syllables accented on the first.

Lā' dy	măn ly	fin ish	frost y
sha dy	can dy	pit y	dust y
ti dy	in step	win try	nut meg
i vy	en vy	cob web	pub lish
du ty	plen ty	pol ish	pun ish
tu mult	self ish	bon fire	ut most

LESSON XXXI.

Charles and the Dove.

The dove has left the cage.
She will fly to the wood.
She loves to be free.
Charles has not had her long.
He found the dove on the ground. She was hurt.

He took pity on the dove. He put her in the cage. He was kind to her. Now she is well, he lets her go. Charles is glad to see her go. He is a good boy. We should be kind like Charles.

LESSON XXXII.

Words of two syllables accented on the second.

Be hāve′	a like	a fär	re pent
en grave	a bode	a larm	de test
a bide	be hold	de part	ad mit
pro vide	pro mote	re gard	en list
de file	re mote	a mĕnd	a loft
re vile	re buke	in vent	up on
a live	con sume	pre vent	in sult

LESSON XXXIII.

Words in which c sounds like s.

cēde	āce	īce	sprūce	cĕnt
cīte	rāce	nīce	trūce	cĕll

Words in which c sounds like k.

cāke	cold	clove	căn	cot
cape	cope	cube	camp	cub
cave	core	cure	clod	cut

Words in which g sounds like j.

gĕm	gĭll	pāge	chānge	hĭnge
gĭn	gībe	rāge	rānge	frĭnge

Words in which g sounds as in gate.

gāle	grind	glăd	rig	rug
game	gold	gag	big	gum
glide	gore	tag	hug	gust

LESSON XXXIV.

thē	thĭs	with	thorn.	ring
thy	that	thank	thump	long
those	thus	theft	bang	sung

---

chăt	chub	hatch	ârch	scale
chest	chump	fetch	chāfe	scold
check	bench	ditch	chide	scene
chin	pinch	notch	choke	scŭd
chop	punch	crutch	porch	scrub

LESSON XXXV.

Words of two syllables accented on the first.

Bĕl' fry	emp ty	com pend	vàr nish
pan try	den tist	bod y	tar nish
dan dy	rel ish	rad ish	bā by
brand ish	ob long	sul try	na vy
band box	trust y	sun dry	va ry
cap tive	pros pect	burn ish	safe ty
en try	ol ive	turn pike	du ly
ban ish	act ive	strip ling	fu ry
dusk y	con cave	dis cord	eve ning
fes tive	bap tist	prod uct	tru ly

LESSON XXXVI.

Jane and the Rose.

This is Jane.
She has a rose in her hand.
It is in full bloom.
She took it from that bush.
She got it for a lady.
The lady was kind to Jane,
and gave her a good book.

Jane did not forget this. The lady will thank her for the rose, and Jane will be happy.

We should not forget those that do us good. We should be glad to do them good, and to make them happy.

LESSON XXXVII.

Words of two syllables accented on the second.

A sīde	ex tĕnd	be fit	a non
be side	de cant	be long	de fend
con trive	up set	be yond	ex pect
im bibe	ab surd	dis turb	e volve
de ride	a drift	con-sult	ex pand
con fide	a mid	con tend	ex pend
de scribe	o mit	con volve	in fest
in scribe	por tend	re volt	re gret

LESSON XXXVIII.

Tāste	glebe	bold	bland	bent	brisk
chaste	wide	fold	blank	blend	cling
haste	blind	hold	brand	elk	clink
paste	find	fort	belt	end	crisp
baste	hind	bănd	bend	blink	link
waste	kind	hank	best	brink	fond

font	pond	blush	brush	clang	crest
pomp	blunt	brunt	bump	cramp	cleft

Let the scholar be requested to give examples of some of the words in this lesson, which contain *a* sounding as in hate; *e* as in here; *i* as in mine; *o* as in globe; *a* as in hat; *e* as in pen; *i* as in pin; *o* as in not; *u* as in nut.

LESSON XXXIX.

Mĭld	most	cȧst	crănk	hank	held
child	bolt	craft	damp	lamp	ding
mind	jolt	darn	fang	shelf	dish
wind	ford	farm	flank	elm	disk
rind	pork	fast	frank	fend	drift
wild	port	garb	gang	flesh	drink
pint	sport	gasp	gland	fresh	fling
host	old	grasp	hand	heft	flint

Repeat inquiries similar to those on the preceding lesson, and add, " give examples of some words that contain *a* as in bar."

LESSON XL.

Sŏng	bulb	curl	film	land	melt
proug	bulk	curve	fish	lank	mend
strong	bunch	dung	fist	pang	nest
thong	burn	drunk	frisk	plank	next
throng	clump	dump	grist	prank	pelf
romp	crump	durst	hilt	rank	pelt
solve	curb	dusk	hint	samp	pent
soft	curd	dust	hist	sand	went

LESSON XLI.

Brȧve	băn	den	bid	blot	bug
ape	bat	fen	bit	clot	but
crape	brag	glen	brim	clog	club
cráve	bran	ken	clip	crop	cud
flake	cag	then	crib	dot	drŭb
bind	clam	let	dig	got	drum
spike	clan	leg	dim	drop	dub

LESSON XLII.

poor. food.

The Blind Man and his Dog.

That old man is blind.
He is led by a dog.
He calls his dog Trip.
Trip loves the blind old man;
   and he loves Trip too.
That boy is Frank.
He is not a selfish boy.

He takes pity on the poor man, and gives him some food. Frank thinks the man wants it more than himself.

Trip wants some food too. The old man will give him a part. Trip will frisk and be glad. We should be kind like Frank, and help the poor.

LESSON XLIII.

Grāpe	crăm	shed	fig	hop	scår
grave	crab	shred	fit	lop	star
lave	crag	sled	glib	mob	par
nape	dam	stem	grim	nod	jar
pave	drag	them	grit	not	arc
strife	fag	step	hid	mop	barn
strike	fan	wed	hip	plod	barb
strive	fat	bet	if	plot	yarn

LESSON XLIV.

Stămp	slang	tank	helm	jest	lest
scalp	stand	tramp	help	kept	guest
shalt	strand	apt	helve	lend	wept
shank	pang	desk	hemp	pest	dwelt

ink	milk	fund	hurl	musk	send
king	milt	grunt	hush	plump	sent
lift	imp	gulf	hurt	prompt	shelve
limp	burst	gulp	husk	rend	smelt
lint	crust	hump	lump	rent	swept
lisp	flush	hung	lust	rest	spend
list	furl	hunt	must	self	tend

LESSON XLV.

Words of two syllables accented on the first.

Gĕn′ try	per ish	stock ing	dū ring
im pulse	res tive	stur dy	glo ry
flesh y	scur vy	sub urb	wa ry
par ish	sen try	sur ly	bru tish
van ish	con clāve	trib une	ju ry
pel try	in cest	fur long	ze nith
fret ful	sin ful	pot ash	là zy

Repeat the inquiries on lessons 38 and 39, and add, " mention some words that contain u as in cube." Repeat these inquiries in the following lessons, till the scholar is familiar with the sounds of the vowels; and make him familiar, also, with the marks used to denote them.

LESSON XLVI.
The Moon and Stars.

It is evening.
See the moon rise.
It is round and full.
How it mounts up in the sky.
John can see to come home.
He was sent to the town, and
told to be in haste.

So he did not stop at all, but came as fast as he could. How dark it would be without the moon and stars. God makes the moon shine. He makes the stars shine too. We should love God for this

LESSON XLVII.

Words of two syllables, accented on the second.

Sub lime´	ab scŏnd	pre tend	cra vat
as cribe	a long	de spond	a bet
be hind	a mendṣ	re but	be set
de spite	rat an	re lapse	ad just
de rive	be twixt	re volve	a bash
de prive	con vulse	re spond	e nact
for sake	de volve	trans mit	sub tract
per fume	him self	fo meṇt	dis tract
sub scribe	per haps	e vent	e rect
de prave	de pict	en camp	a dult
sur vive	in flict	im pend	al cove

LESSON XLVIII.

Words of two syllables, accented on the first.

Grāte´ ful	făm ish	test y	lil y
bale ful	lav ish	vest ry	bash ful
gra vy	brack ish	ver dict	priv y
on ly	rav ish	rel ict	brim stone
past ry	ad junct	cher ish	in sect
pru dish	ab ject	blem ish	thrift y
sli my	as pect	ver y	dis trict
po ny	bank rupt	con sort	in stinct
wi ly	oc tave	con junct	cit y
co hort	con tact	cos tive	glob ūle

LESSON XLIX.

Rāve	slave	bile	drive	gad	lad
safe	stave	bride	fife	gap	lag
save	tape	clime	file	had	lap
scrape	wave	crime	hide	hag	jet
shape	bate	dime	flăp	hap	let
shave	bide	dive	flat	have	met

pet	beg	nip	rip	grub	plum
fret	leg	prig	scrip	grum	plug
tret	keg	prim	ship	hut	plunge
set	lid	rid	sip	lug	pug
wet	mid	rim	glut	mum	rug

LESSON L.

Jane and the Plums.

See that plum-tree.
It is behind the wall.
It is full of nice ripe plums.
Jane looks at the plums, and
  wants some of them.
She asks Charles to get her
  some.

She forgets that they do not belong to her.
Charles tells her so, and that he must not take
them. He is a good boy. Jane thanks him.
Now she has no wish for the plums. She would
not take them if she could. We should not
wish to take things that do not belong to us.

LESSON LI.

Hăsh	tent	mint	loft	lung	årm
cash	test	mist	oft	rush	are
dash	text	pink	cost	rusk	hasp
gash	vend	prink	frog	rust	lard
lash	vent	print	frost	scurf	last
clash	vest	rift	froth	slump	marl
flash	weld	risk	pulp	stump	marsh
splash	welt	scrimp	pump	stunt	mart
slash	wend	shift	pulse	thrush	mast
mash	west	shrift	purl	thrust	past
smash	zest	shrimp	churl	thump	raft
rash	desk	shrink	rung	trump	scarf

LESSON LII.

Words of two syllables, accented on the first.

Hăp′ py	jol ly	sab bath	tal ly
ed dy	skit tish	clam my	tab by
fer ry	bon ny	cur ry	fop pish
hob by	lob by	snap pish	sun ny
hur ry	hol ly	chal lenge	slop py
dal ly	cher ry	sul ly	mum my
dit ty	ber ry	pen ny	pup py
flur ry	mer ry	pop py	sor ry
tar ry	ral ly	fin ny	sot tish
wit ty	sil ly	hub bub	her ring
jel ly	rub bish	car ry	sal ly
chub by	put ty	mar ry	shrub by
pet ty	off ing	rud dy	pud ding
ef fort	mam moth	pet tish	star ry

LESSON LIII.

Words of two syllables, accented on the second.

Ar rīve′	com mánd	as sist	ac cept
as sume	ac cĕnt	suc cinct	cor rect
com mune	al lot	ef fect	ap pend
con nive	oc cult	con nect	ar rest
il lume	col lect	at tend	of fend
pol lute	col lapse	at tempt	sup plant
com mute	com mend	ad dict	dis sect
op pugn	af fect	com mit	at test
ar range	at tract	af flict	ac cost
al lude	at tach	dis sent	cor rupt

LESSON LIV.

Words having the sound of or, as in nor.

nor	for	north	lorn
or	fork	morn	lord

cord	thorn	for lorn	re tort
cork	born	as sort	es cort
corn	orb	ex tort	dis gorge
corpse	scorn	sub orn	re córd
sort	short	ab hor	re form
stork	snort	de form	in form
form	torch	dis tort	con form
storm	scorch	ab sorb	trans form
gorge	ac cord'	per form	ab sorb' ent
horn	a dorn	re sort	a bor tive

LESSON LV.

walk.   be come'.

The lame Man and the bad Boys.

That poor man walks with a
　　cane.
It helps him to walk.
His foot is bent out of shape,
　　and he is quite lame.
He limps as he walks.
See the boys that stand by
him.   They are not good boys.   They make
sport of the lame man.   He looks sad, and I pity
him.   He did not make himself lame.   God
made him so.   He was born with a bent foot.
He is not to blame for it.

These boys would be sorry to be made sport
of, if they should become lame.   I hope they
will think of this, and do so no more.   Only
bad boys make sport of those that they should
pity and help.

LESSON LVI.

Skāte	fate	lathe	bake	take	stage
date	bathe	swathe	make	age	sage

quite	rive	June	lamb	limb	rob
life	scribe	puke	pad	slip	rod
like	slide	rule	pan	sprig	rot
blithe	slime	huge	pat	strip	scot
mile	smile	măd	gnat	swig	shop
pike	thrive	map	shrank	swim	shot
pride	tide	mat	crept	tip	sob
prime	tile	nag	slept	skip	throb
ride	duke	nap	ship	pot	job
rife	fume	jamb	slim	prop	jot

LESSON LVII.

Shărp	blĕd	sing	bulge	trash	midst
scarp	fed	sink	trunk	crash	wing
shaft	tempt	skim	trust	sash	wind
smart	sect	sling	jump	gnash	wink
snarl	lens	spring	shrunk	lapse	wish
sparse	wrest	sting	just	act	wisp
start	sift	wring	tuft	fact	wist
vast	silk	singe	turf	tract	jilt
waft	tilt	cringe	tush	lent	guilt
charm	tint	tinge	tusk	scent	prism
chart	twist	twinge	duct	delve	wrong
harsh	wilt	bilge	wrung	else	wroth

LESSON LVIII.
Words ending in ll and l.

Bĕll	spell	shall	chill	shrill
ell	tell	mall	thill	thrill
dell	quell	ill	kill	trill
cell	well	bill	skill	sill
fell	yell	dill	mill	till
knell	dwell	fill	pill	still
shell	swell	gill	drill	quill
smell	sell	hill	frill	squill

will	gull	ca bal′	ex pel	dis till′ }
swill	hull	ca nal	pro pel	dis til }
spill	lull	ex cel	re bel	in still }
rill	null	re pel	ex tol	in stil }
doll	skull	im pel	un til	ful fill }
loll	cull	com pel	an nul	ful fil }
scull	dull	dis pel	ho tel	fŏre tell

Monosyllables end in *ll*, if preceded by a single vowel; and if not, they end in *l*.

Most, and probably all the dissyllables in common use, (except proper names,) that end in *ll*, are to be found in Lessons 58, 67, 92, and 96; viz. distill, instill, fulfill, patroll, enroll, controll, (which are sometimes spelt with one *l*,) foretell, bridewell, recall, befall, inthrall, install, and appall.

LESSON LIX.

Tru′ ant.   does.   school.   girl.   play.

The Truant Boy.

Look at that boy.
I will not tell his name; for he is a lazy boy, and does not love to go to school.
He should be in school now.
The bell rung at nine.
It is past the time, and the school has begun. He has a fish-pole and line. He is going to fish in the brook. How he looks around him. He thinks somebody may see him, and tell the man that keeps the school. God sees him, and he should think of that too. He is doing wrong. He will not be so happy in his sport, as he would be in school. Good boys and girls do not play truant.

LESSON LX.

Words of three syllables, accented on the second.

| A bŏl′ ish | as ton ish | ac com plish |
| ad mon ish | de mol ish | es tab lish |

em bel lish	pre ṣump tive	pre ven tive
re plen ish	se duc tive	in cen tive
ex tin guish	pre scrip tive	de cep tive
dis tin guish	vin dic tive	pre cep tive
re lin quish	at ten tive	re ten tive
di min ish.	con sump tive	sub junc tive
as ṣem bly	in vec tive	un rū ly
de struc tive	per spec- tive	in qui ry
de scrip tive	pro spec tive	pro mo tive

LESSON LXI.

Words in the plural number.

Bănds	elks	flints	ponds	curls	skātes
lads	elms	figs	hops	nuts	grapes
clams	nests	lids	lots	clubs	miles
crabs	dens	ships	horns	drums	bones
maps	steps	wings	dogs	lumps	mules

In which of these words has *s*, at the end, the sound of *z* ?

LESSON LXII.

Gāte	climb	vălve	twig	swing	with ⎫
slate	guide	thrash	twin	slit	withe ⎬
mate	tithe	tact	chin	spit·	smith
wage	writhe	champ	shin	split	frith
gauge ⎫	scythe ⎫	cant	skin	quit	quilt
gage ⎬	sythe ⎬	scant	spin	flit	squib
knave	shore	plant	grin	knit	squint
guile	store	rant	swift	filth	trim
chime	truth.	van	quip	thin	width

LESSON LXIII.

Bārge	carve	lath	scăb.	strap	debt
charge	harm	path	scan	spasm	depth
large	harp	baths	scrap	wrap	length
blast	gape	laths	stab	adz	strength
carp	bath	paths	stag	wren	glimpse

build	chink	broth	knot	strut	dumb
built	pith	cloth	spot	thrum	thumb
stint	stilt	cloths	troth	scud	plumb
string	kiln	bronze	sculk)	stud	numb
thing,	hymn	moth	skulk)	shun	crumb
think	stop	moths	scum	stun	be numb'
thrift	strop	knob	shrub	buzz	suc cumb

LESSON LXIV.

Lit' tle.   who.   care.   keep.   Bi' ble.

The Little Lamb.

Who takes care of the little lamb ?

The sheep takes care of it.

Who takes care of the sheep?

The boy takes care of her.

Who takes care of the boy ?

The man who is his father.

Who takes care of the man? God takes care of the man. God takes care of us all. He is very good. He keeps us in life. He gives us food and clothes. He gives us all good things. We should think of this. We should love God. We should wish to do his will. We should do all that he tells us to do in the Bible.

LESSON LXV.

Words of two syllables accented on the second.

Be tīde'	pre side	im pugn	pre dict
sub side	di vide	be sides	ac quit
re vive	re port	de cide	per mit
es cape	re sume	ex cĕpt	de sist
con jure	re side	a dept	in sist
pre scribe	tran scribe	con tempt	in volve
pre sume	di vine	sub mit	di gest

di vest	sub sist	sus pect	re tard
jap an	tre pan	in fect	pla card
per sist	ab rupt	e lect	im part
e lapse	in fract	e quip	dis charge
a dapt	re fract	for bid	ci gar
se dan	com pact	ce ment	em bark
a dopt	sub ject	por tent	re mand
ab solve	de fect	de bar	de mand

LESSON LXVI.

Words containing the diphthongs oi and oy.

Troy	choice	em broil	cŏn' voy
roil	voice	pur loin	en voy
coil	re joice'	tur moil	in voice
foist	ad join	ex ploit	mem oir
groin	a droit	de coy	boil er
joist	a noint	en joy	clois ter
quoit	ap point	al loy	vīce roy
foil	a void	em ploy	e' qui poişe
noişe	de spoil	an noy	va' ri o loid
poişe	de void	de stroy	reş er voir'

LESSON LXVII.

Words of two syllables, accented on the first.

Slāv' ish	post script	gang way	ar my
e dict	bi ped	gen tile	craft y
pre cinct	ho ly	land scape	dar ling
home spun	a pish	mist y	far thing
que ry	mi ry	bant ling	gar nish
pa thos	ju rist	con script	har py
pre text	luke warm	off spring	sar caşm
pre cept	fŭr bish	ram part	tar dy
bride well	ug ly	im pōst	har dy
tru işm	ex ile	prox y	pas time
the işm	tran script	cop y	pass pōrt
de işm	diph thong	wind pipe	ghast ly

LESSON LXVIII.

Sit' ting.   moth' er.   why.   lie.   you.

The Little Girl who did not tell the Truth.

That little girl is Mary.
She is sitting by her mother.
Why does she cry, and look
   so sad?
She has done wrong.
She has not told the truth.
She has told a lie.

She found a cent, and put it in her bag. Her
mother had lost it. She told Mary to come to
her.

Mary, have you found the cent? No, mother,
I have not. Give me that bag. See, here is the
cent, and you found it. You have told me a lie.
I am very sorry. You have done wrong. I must
punish you. You cannot go to ride with Charles
and James. You must stay at home. I hope
you will be sorry too, and ask God to forgive
you, and help you to do so no more.

LESSON LXIX.

Words ending in áck, ac, eck, ick, ock, and uck.

Băck	snack	quack	ma ni ac
hack	pack	thwack	ål ma nac
jack	rack	bar' rack	e lē' gi ac
lack	crack	ran sack	de mo ni ac
black	knack	knap sack	bĕck
clack	track	at tack'	deck
slack	sack	lĭ' lac *	check
smack	stack	zo' di ac	neck

peck	trick	pock	mat tock
speck	sick	rock	but tock
wreck	tick	crock	cas sock
be deck'	stick	frock	hav ock
thick	quick	sock	buck
kick	wick	stock	duck
lick	knock	pēa' cock	chuck
click	cock	hăd dock	luck
slick	dock	pad lock	cluck
pick	hock	wed lock	pluck
rick	shock	hil lock	muck
brick	lock	bŭl lock	suck
crick	block	hĕm lock	truck
chick	clock	fet lock	struck
nick	flock	ham mock	tuck
prick	mock	ban nock	stuck

Which words end in ac, and which of the dissyllables in ack, and ock ! Are not these the only dissyllables in common use that end in ack and ock ! Do any monosyllables end in c? Are there any words in common use that end in ick, except frolick, traffick !

LESSON LXX.

Words ending in ch, che, and tch.

Stàrch	clinch	such	wàtch	pitch
parch	flinch	church	ĕtch	stitch
larch	linch	lurch	sketch	witch
march	inch	os' trich	stretch	switch
drĕnch	winch	batch	ketch	twitch
stench	filch	catch	vetch	botch
trench	milch	thatch	wretch	scotch
wench	perch	latch	retch	blotch
wrench	lunch	match	itch	crutch
quench	hunch	snatch	bitch	clutch
rich	munch	patch	hitch	dis patch' }
niche	much	scratch	flitch	de spatch }

What word ends in iche ? Ch is sometimes preceded by a long vowel or diphthong, as in beech, teach Is not tch always preceded by a short vowel ;

LESSON LXXI.

Words ending in sĭve and cĭve.

Măs′ sive	dif fu sive	of fen sive
pas sive	co he sive	ex ten sive
mis sive	ad he sive	ex pen sive
pen sive	e va sive	ex ces sive
con dū′ cive	de ci sive	pro gres sive
a bu sive	cor ro sive	op pres sive
de lu sive	per sua sive	ex pres sive
in clu sive	dis sua sive	suc ces sive
e lu sive	co ĕr cive	re spon sive
ex clu sive	sub ver sive	sub mis sive
il lu sive	ex cur sive	com pul sive
in tru sive	dis cur sive	re pul sive
con clu sive	ex pan sive	com pre hen′ sive
ob tru sive	de fen sive	ap pre hen sive

What two words end in *cive?* Are not all others, ending with this sound, spelt *sive?*

LESSON LXXII.

Grain.   wheel.   wa′ ter.   bolt′ ed.   sis′ ter.   bread.   bowl.

The Grist-mill.

Here is a mill.
It stands by the brook.
We call it a grist-mill, be-
    cause grain is ground in it.
How fast the wheel turns
    round.
The water makes the wheel
go.   The wheel makes the stones go, that are
inside of the mill.   The stones grind the grain,
and make it fine.   The grain is bolted, and made
into flour.   The boy must carry it home.   His

sister will make it into bread. In the morning, he will have some of it in a nice bowl of milk. Do you not love bread and milk?

LESSON LXXIII.
Words of two syllables, accented on the second.

Con sist'	ob ject	be troth	pre şent
ab stract	bi sect	di vulge	re şolve
de tract	de tect	pro mulge	re şult
ex tract	con vict	in dulge	re quest
con tract	con flict	de tach	con test
re tract	re strict	re trench	con demn
pro tract	dis tinct	as cend	con tent
se lect	ex tinct	tran scend	in tent
re flect	con coct	as cent	a venge
in flect	con duct	de scend	re venge
per fect	de duct	de scent	in fringe
neg lect	in duct	fer ment	im pinge
re spect	in struct	tor ment	ex punge
in spect	con struct	re cant	re pulse
sus pect	ob struct	des cant	e clipse
di rect	ex tent	con trast	be quest
e ject	la ment	mo lest	ex chänge
in ject	re mit	pro test	de range
re ject	e mit	ro tund	es trange
pro tect	çha grin	re lent	pro scribe
pro ject	ro bust	re şent	van dyke

LESSON LXXIV.
Words of two syllables, accented on the first.

Nä' tive	grace ful	sўr inge	plen ty
da tive	dole ful	loz enge	knurl y
mo tive	wa vy	stin gy	stud y
vo tive	whol ly	dam ask	sulk y
a corn	pre fect	or ange	com bat

con quest	lust y	lin guist *	skill ful)
scant ling	lamb kin	dis junct	skil ful
pig my	van quish	for tune	will ful)
kid nap	an guish *	prov erb	wil ful)
loft y	lan guish *	gris ly	am bush
sol emn	hun gry *	wish ful	bul rush
bran dy	an gry *	scorn ful	bul wark

  * These words are pronounced as if the first syllables ended with g, as ang guish, &c.

LESSON LXXV.

Words ending in double consonants, with others in which ough has the sound of ŭf.

Bŭtt	staff	doff	puff	re buff
add	quaff	buff	gruff	dis' taff
ebb	cliff	cuff	stuff	mas tiff
egg	skiff	huff	ruff	sher iff
jagg	miff	luff	rough	tar iff
inn	stiff	bluff	tough	pon tiff
odd	off	muff	slough	bail iff
chaff	scoff	snuff	e nough'	plain tiff

Which of these words end in *ough?*

LESSON LXXVI.

Words ending in o, with others in which oa, ow, ew, ough, eau, owe, and oe have the sound of ō, as in globe.

Cär' go	ty ro	ver ti go	si roc co
quär to	co coa	buff a lo	mo roc co
hē ro	căn to	em bry o	me ment o
ne gro	mot to	pōr ti co	mu lat to
ve to	grot to	tor pe' do	em bär go
ha lo	jun to	vol ca no	man i fest' o
bra vo	sal vo	po ta to	bow
ze ro	stuc co	oc ta vo	low
tri o	cal' i co	pro vi so	blow
so lo	in di go	to băc co	flow

glow	shad ow	win now	ål though'
mow	wid ow	ar row	fŭr' lough
show }	wind ow	bar row	fur low }
shew }	fal low	far row	beau
snow	shal low	har row	bū' ʙeau
*k*now	sal low	mar row	ba teau'
row	tal low	nar row	pōrt măn' teau
throw	cal low	spar row	owe
crow	bel low	bor row	doe
grow	fel low	mor row	woe }
tow	mel low	sor row	wo }
strow	yel low	bur row	toe
sow	bil low	fur row	foe
stow	pil low	be low'	hoe
slow	wil low	be stow	sloe
sew	fol low	dough	roe
ĕl' bow	min now	though	throe

Which word ends in *oa?* What words end in *ough?* What in *eau?*
In *owe?* In *oe?*

Plurals which end in *oes.*

Wōeş	bra voeş	cal i coeş	mu lăt toeş
cår' gōeş	ne groeş	po tā' toeş	em băr goeş
hē roeş	bŭff' a loeş	vol ca noeş	man i fĕst' oeş

LESSON LXXVII.

Swore.   throw.   swear.   vain.

The Boy that Swore.

It is noon.
The school is out.
Those boys are playing ball.
See the boy that has the bat
in his hand.
His name is Robert.
He shakes the bat at the boy
who stands by him. He is angry at the boy.

Why is he angry? The boy did not throw the ball right. Robert did not hit it, and he lost his turn. That made him angry. He scolds his playmate. He swears at him. He takes the name of God in vain. It is wrong to do so—very wrong. God forbids us to swear. That man tells Robert it is wrong. He tells him to stop. I hope he will stop, and swear no more. If boys swear, you must not do like them, but tell them it is wrong.

LESSON LXXVIII.

Words of three syllables accented variously.

Rĕl' a tive	gal van işm	con tra dict'
neg a tive	scant i ly	in ter dict
nar ra tive	priv a tive	in ter sect
car a van	vóc a tive	in ter mit
cat a ract	in fa my	com pre hend
con tra band	in fan try	cor re spond
ap a thy	mal a dy	ap pre hend
par a sol	mor al ist	rep re hend
big a my	sub tra hend	un der stand
san a tive	vag a bond	rep re şent
lax a tive	in fan tile	in ter cept
sed a tive	os tra cişm	in ter rupt
bot a nist	ped ant ry	rec ol lect
prof it less	dram a tist	cir cum vent
çhiv al ry *	sym pa thy	vi o lin
dog ma tişm	par al lel	rec on cile
gal ax y	pen al ty	im por tune
tam a rind	tyr an ny	op por tune
tan ta mount	log a rithm	co in cide

* Some pronounce tshiv' al re.

In this lesson, and in lessons 117, 118, 133, 161, 162, 164, 171, 173, 174, 175, 176, and those ending in *ble* only, (pages 132—4,) the principal difficulty in spelling lies in the syllable immediately preceding or succeeding the accented one, and to this the attention of both teacher and scholar should be particularly directed. The teacher, also, in reviewing would do well to put out the words indiscriminately from the different columns.

LESSON LXXIX.

Words ending in x and xe.

Flăx	bō′ rax	sўn tax	per plex
tax	tho rax	ver tex	trans fix
lax	cli max	vor tex	crū′ ci fix
wax	a pex	com plex	e qui nox
ax	re flex	con vex	păr a dox
sex	ra dix	in dex	or tho dox
mix	pro lix	suf fix	par al lax
six	pre fix	af fix	cĭr cum flex
ox	phe nix	con flux	ap pĕn′ dix
box	la rynx	in flux	tes tā trix
flux	pha lanx	an nex′	hĕt′ e ro dox

Do any other words, in common use, end in x, than those in this lesson?

LESSON LXXX.

Words containing the diphthongs ou and ow.

Couch	spout	pounce	mouth
vouch	doubt	wound *	mouths
pouch	lout	sound	south
slouch	gouge	snout	mouth
crouch	lounge	trout	bough
pound	douse	sour	plough ⎫
foul	drought	hour	plow ⎬
gout	louse	mouse	slough
flout	noun	spouse	thou
scour	our	rouse	a bound′
scout	ounce	sprout	a bout
bout	bounce	route * ⎫	ac count
shroud	flounce	rout* ⎬	a mount

* Some pronounce the ou as o in move.

a round	de vout	growl	flow er
as tound	re doubt	howl	low er
ca rouse	boun' ty	scowl	pow er
con found	count er	prowl	show er
sur round	coun ty	brown	tow er
sur mount	found ling	clown	dow ry
a rouse	floun der	crown	flow ret
es pouse	păr' a mount	town	row en
com pound	en count' er	browse	pow der
ex pound	ren count er	drowse	cow ard
pro pound	count er mănd'	bow' el	cow herd
pro found	vow	tow el	cow slip
re dound	bow	trow el	al low'
re sound	mow	vow el	a vow
a vouch	brow	bow er	en dow
de nounce	prow	cow er	re nown
de vour	sow	dow er	em pow' er

LESSON LXXXI.

Sail.   three.   a cross'.   deep.   climb' ing.   sail' or.
France.   what.   car' ried.   cot' ton.   ex' change.

The Ship.

How fast that ship sails.
Do you see those three tall
    poles ?
We call them masts.
Across the masts are the
    yards.
The sails stretch along the
yards. The men pull the sails with ropes. The
sails catch the wind, as it blows, and the wind
drives the ship along in the deep water. A man
is climbing up some ropes, that look like a ladder.
We call them shrouds. He is a sailor. The ship

has come from France, and is full of silks and cloths. What did she carry to France? She carried bales of cotton. We have more of this than we want, and they have more silks and cloths than they want. So we let them have cotton, and they let us have silks and cloths. We exchange with them. This is trade, or commerce.

LESSON LXXXII.

Words in which ou, o, and oo have the sound of ŭ as in sun.

Young	word	oth er	son ship
touch	worm	col or	stom ach
scourge	worse	come ly	ton nage
coun´ try	worst	com fort	thor *ough*
cour age	wort	com pass	work man
cous in	wont	cov er	wont ed
coup let	sponge	cov ert	won der
doub let	tong*ue*	cov et	won drous
flour ish	bom*b*	cov ey	wor ry
nour ish	one (wun)	coz en	wor ship
coup le	once (wunce)	doz en	wor thy
doub le	none *	gov ern	worth less
troub le	monk	hon ey	a bove´
troub lous	doth	mon ey	af front
jour ney	dost	mon grel †	a mong
jour nal	flood	monk ey	a mongst
south ern	blood	noth ing	at tor´ ney
south ward	blood´ y	ov en	an oth er
so journ	blood shed	plov er	bom bast ic
ad journ´	bom bast	pom mel	dis com fit
court´ e ous	bor *ough*	shov el	pome gran ate
court e sy	broth er	slov en	col´ an der
courte sy	moth er	smoth er	com pa ny

* Some pronounce nōne.   † Pronounced mŭng´ grel.

con jur er	cov et ous	whor tle ber ry
con sta ble	sov er *eign*	ef front' er y
cov e nant	love li ness	wor' ship per }
cov er let	drom' e da ry	wor ship er }

LESSON LXXXIII.

Words in which u and ui have the sound of ū as in cube.

Lūte	de pute	con' sti tute	res o lute
flute	im pute	des ti tute	sub sti tute
brute	com pute	dis so lute	suit
a cute'	re pute	ex e cute	suite *
con fute	dis pute	in sti tute	fruit
sa lute	re fute	per se cute	bruit
di lute	trib' ute	pros e cute	pur suit'
trans mute	stat ute	pros ti tute	re cruit

* Some pronounce swēt.

Juice	ob tuse	in duce	a buse
sluice	rĕf' use	con duce	con fuse
cruse }	spruce	pro duce	ac cuse
cruise }	truce	in tro duce'	dif fuse
use	ad duce'	use	ex cuse
a buse'	tra duce	muse	re fuse
ex cuse	e duce	fuse	af fuse
dif fuse	de duce	bruise	in fuse
re cluse	re duce	cruise	pe ruse
ab struse	se duce	a muse'	suf fuse

What words end in uite, uit, uice, uise, and uise ? Which words are spelt alike and pronounced differently ?

LESSON LXXXIV.

Words in which a, ea, ai, and ei have the sound of ā as in hate.

Lāke	flake	slake	brake
shake	snake	spake	drake

ke	çhi cane	com plain	cam paign′
ake	count′ er pane	ex plain	çham paign
take	hŭr ri cane	re main	ar raign
ake	chain	do main	deign
wake′	plain	re frain	feign
ir take	main	ob tain	reign
paque ⎫	slain	con strain	came
pake ⎭	pain	de tain	lame
reak	rain	re tain	name
eak	brain	main tain	dame
che (āke)	drain	con tain	fame
ane	lain	per tain	shame
ane ′	grain	ab stain	blame
ine	strain	at tain	flame
lane	train	sus tain	frame
nane	sprain	pŏr′ ce lain	same
rane	stain	ap per tain′	tame
ane	twain	as cer tain	aim
ane	vain	en ter tain	claim
vane	wain	skein	maim
nĕm′ brane	swain	rein	ac claim′
iu mane′	gain	vein	de claim
n sane	chĭl′ blain	feint	re claim
oro fane	or dain′	reins	pro claim
ir bane	diş dain	hei′ nous	ex claim

Which word ends in *aque!* Which in *che!* What words in *eak!* in *tign!* in *eign!* What end in, or contain *ein!*

LESSON LXXXV.

In the following words g sounds as in gate, go, gun.

Gĭft	gig	girt	gim let ⎫
gimp	gild	gĕt	gim blet ⎭
give	gĭrd	gēar	gid dy
gilt	girl	geese	giz zard
gill	girth	gĭg′ gle	gĭr dle

trĭg ger	crag gy	mau ger)	for give
dag ger	shag gy	mau gre)	dog' ger el
stag, ger	wag gish	mēa ger)	wag ger y̆
swag ger	fog gy	mea gre)	to geth' er
crag ged	drug gist	ea ger	an' ger *
shag ged	slug gish	tăr get	fin ger
dog ged	gew gaw	be gĕt'	lin ger
rug ged	tī ger	for get	hun ger
rag ged	ău ger	be gin	lon ger

* The first syllable in this and the following words is pronounced as if it ended with g.

LESSON LXXXVI.

Win' ter. be' gins. farm' er. horse. deep. car' ries. hop' ping.

The Planting.

The winter is past.
It begins to be warm.
The farmer ploughs his land.
His son drives the horse.
The plough turns up the ground, and makes deep furrows.

Then he plants the corn. The sun shines. The showers fall. The blades spring up, and grow fast. The farmer must take care of his corn. He ploughs the ground once more. He hoes out the weeds, and makes little hills around the blades. Look at that black bird. What is he doing in the furrow? He follows the farmer in his work, and picks up the small worms. He carries them to his nest, and gives them to the young birds for food. He will soon be back to get more, hopping about in the furrow. Do not

kill him. It is wrong; for he does much good
to the farmer. He destroys the worms that
would hurt the corn.

LESSON LXXXVII.

Words in which ay, ey, ei, and ai have the sound of ā as in
hate.

Bāy	stray	Wedneş day*	in veigh'
day	say	Thurş day*	neigh' bor
faÿ	stay	Fri day*	paint
gay	way	Sat' ur day*	faint
hay	sway	yĕs ter day	plaint
jay	de cay'	hol y day	saint
lay	de lay	sley	taint
clay	re lay	they	quaint
flay	al lay	whey	faith
play	dis play	dey	waist
slay	dis may	bey	waive†
may	de fray	prey	dai' ly
nay	ar ray	hey' day	dain ty
pay	be tray	pur vey'	dai ry
ray	por tray	o bey	dai şy
bray	a stray	con vey	rai ment
dray	as say	sur vey	ac quaint'
fray	es say	sur vey' or	at taint
gray	be wray	con vey ance	com plaint
pray	Sun' day*	neigh	con straint
spray	Mon day*	weigh	dis traint
tray	Tueş day*	sleigh	re straint

* In these words ay sounds obscurely. † Some, wave.
What words end in, or contain ey? What eigh?

LESSON LXXXVIII.

Words in which a, ai, ei, and ao have the sound of ā as in hate.

Vāle	bale	male	sale
ale	hale	pale	tale

stale	trail	blade	ti rade
wale	sail	glade	cŏm′ rade
re gale′	tail	made	bar ri cade′
in hale	vail ⎫	spade	ser e nade
im pale ⎫	veil ⎭	trade	lem on ade
em pale ⎭	quail	wade	can non ade
ail	wail	bro cade′	col on nade
bail	frail′ ty	cas cade	mas quer ade
fail	sail or	ar cade	ret ro grade
hail	tail or	bri gade	bal us trade
jail ⎫	as sail′	cock ade	pal i sade
gaol*⎭	de tail	block ade	cav al cade
jail′ er ⎫	en tail	de grade	prom e nade
gaol er*⎭	re tail	e vade	a fraid′
flail	cur tail	pa rade	up braid
mail	a vail	per vade	maid
nail	pre vail	in vade	aid
snail	fade	per suade	braid
pail	bade	dis suade	laid
rail	shade	cru sade	paid
frail	lade	stock ade	staid

What words end in *aid*? Do any others, with this sound, end in *aid*, except compounds? * Pronounced jāle, jā′ ler.

LESSON LXXXIX.

Words in which a, ai, ea, and ei have the sound of ā as in hate.

Hāte	bait	gait er	eigh teenth
pate	gait	great	eigh ty
rate	plait	straight	in nate
grate	trait	eight	stag nate
prate	strait	weight	tes tate
sate	wait	freight	fil trate
state	a wait′	eighth (āᴛʜ)	frus trate
late	trait′ or	eigh′ teen	dic tate

nar rate	se date	col late	der o gate
or nate	cre ate	cŏl' lo cate	sur ro gate
quăd rate	re late	suf fo cate	per son ate
mī grate	di late	dis lo cate	in to nate
va cate	e late	in vo cate	dec o rate
vi brate	in flate	rev o cate	per fo rate
lo cate	trans late	con vo cate	el e vate
a bate'	es tate	ab ro gate	ren o vate
de bate	mis tate	ar ro gate	ī so late

Which word ends in *eat?* Which in *aight?* What words end in, or contain *eight?* What *ait?* Do any others, with this sound, end in *ait?*

LESSON XC.

Words in which a, ai, ay, ei, e, and ea have the sound of ā as in bare.

Bāre	tare	lair	heir
care	stare	pair	there
scare	square	stair	where
dare	ware	af fair'	ere
fare	wĕl' fare	re pair	there' fore*
hare	de clare'	im pair	where fore
share	pre pare	de spair	bear
flare	com pare	cŏr' sair	pear
glare	a ware	fai ry	tear
mare	be ware	pray er	swear
snare	air	pa rent	wear
pare	fair	ap pa' rent	for bear'
spare	hair	trans pa rent	for swear
rare	chair	their	for bear' ance

* Some pronounce thĕr' fore, whĕr' fore.

Which word contains *ay?* What words end in *eir?* What words end in, or contain, *ere?* What *ear?*

They need much whom nothing will content.
Tell me with whom you go, and I will tell you wha
you do.

LESSON XCI.

Sum' mer.   ri' pens.   lies.   work' ed (workt).   paid.
good' ness.

The Husking.

Now it is summer.
The farmer is getting in his grain.
See the tall corn, how it waves in the wind. Soon the soft silk will be seen, and the corn begin to grow yellow. It ripens fast in the warm sun. It is quite ripe. The farmer and his sons pick it. They carry it home to the barn. They are glad to see it as it lies on the floor. They worked hard to get it, and are well paid for their toil.

The farmer asks some men and boys, to come and help him husk the corn. They are kind, and willing to do it. They come in the evening. As they work, they talk, and sing, and are happy. The farmer entertains them well. He gives them plenty of good food, and pure, sweet water. They want no rum, nor strong drink. He thanks them for helping him, and is grateful to God for his goodness.—They all go home before it is late.

LESSON XCII.

Words in which o, oa, ou, and oo have the sound of ō as in globe.

Glōbe	bode	strode	cor rode
probe	code	trode	in com mode'
robe	mode	fore bode'	ĕp' i sode
ode	rode	ex plode	goad

load	boll	mould er ⎰	blown
road	knoll	mold er ⎱	mown
toad	poll	poul try	known
joke	roll	dome	ope
smoke	scroll	comb	scope
poke	droll	foam	hope
spoke	stroll	loam	slope
broke	toll	roam	mope
stroke	coal	bone	grope
yoke	foal	prone	trope
re voke′	goal	cone	e lope′
in voke	shoal	lone	in ter lope′
pro voke	pa troll′ ⎰	hone	ăn′ te lope
con voke	pa trol ⎱	stone	tel e scope
a woke	en roll ⎰	shone	mī cro scope
croak	en rol ⎱	zone	soap
cloak	con troll ⎰	tone	ghost
soak	con trol ⎱	drone	boast
oak	bowl	throne	coast
dole	soul	a tone′	roast
pole	mould ⎰	loan	toast
sole	mold ⎱	moan	broach
stole	moult ⎰	roan	coach
whole	molt ⎱	groan	roach
pa role′	yolk	own	ap proach′
ca jole	sold	shown	en croach
con dole	told	flown	re proach
con sole	shoul′ der	grown	brooch

What words end in *oad*? in *oak*? in *oal*? in *owl*? in *oul*, or contain it?
in *ome*? in *omb*? in *oan*? in *own*? in *ost*? in *ock*?

LESSON XCIII.

Words ending in ōṣe, ōze, ōws, ōẹẹ, and ōse.

Rōṣe	close	hoṣe	proṣe
nose	chose	pose	in cloṣe′

a roṣe	pro poṣe	trans poṣe	gal lowṣ *
de poṣe	im poṣe	in ter poṣe'	close
dis cloṣe	com poṣe	doze	dose
fore cloṣe	op poṣe	ăl' oeṣ	mo rose'
re poṣe	sup poṣe	mal lowṣ	jo cose
ex poṣe	dis poṣe	bel lowṣ *	ver bose

* Some pronounce bĕl' lŭs, găl' lŭs.

What words end in *oze*, in *oeṣ*, and *owṣ*? Which words are spelt alike but pronounced differently?

LESSON XCIV.

Words in which o, oa, oo, and ou have the sound of ō as in globe.

Mōre	forge	course	vote
bore	af ford'	mourn	wrote
lore	sup port	bourn*	de vote'
ore	im port	borne	de note
snore	ex port	worn	ăn' ec dote
score	trans port	shorn	an ti dote
sore	com port	sworn	gross
tore	go' ry	fourth	en gross'
pore	sto ry	gourd	clothe
wore	oar	court	quoth †
swore	roar	cŏn' course	both
yore	hoar	re source'	sloth †
a dore'	soar	dis course	boat
be fore	board	ĭn' ter course	coat
de plore	hoard	horde	bloat
ex plore	coarse	cote	float
im plore	hoarse	dote	gloat
re store	door	mote	goat
cŏm'mo dore	floor	smote	moat
syc a more	four	rote	throat
forth	pour	quote	a float'
sword	source	shote	loaf

* Some pronounce the ou as o in move. † Or, kwŭth, slŏth.

coax	oath	stove	grove
hoax	oaths	clove	throve
loathe	oats.	cove	drove
loath)	loath' some	rove	wove
loth *)	boat swāin *	strove	low' er

* Others pronounce lŏth, bō'sn.

What words end in, or contain *ear?* what *oor?* What end in *rde, ss,*
the?

LESSON XCV.

Words ending in **ase, āss, ace, aze, aize, aşe, aişe,** and **ize.**

Bāse	place	em brace	baize
case	space	dis grace	maize)
chase	brace	re trace	maiz)
vase	grace	gaze	raşe .
bass	trace	haze	phaşe
a base'	de face'	blaze	phraşe
de base	ef face	glaze	păr' a phraşe
e rase	un lace	maze	çhāişe
face	re place	raze	raişe
lace	dis place	craze	praişe
mace	mis place	graze	ap praişe')
pace	gri mace	a maze'	ap prīze)

What words end in *ase* and *āss?* What in *aize,* and *aişe?*

LESSON XCVI.

Words in which a, au; aw, awe, oa, and ou have the sound of
ă as in ball.

Wȧlk	thwart	wa ter
balk	swart	thrall dom)
calk	warmth	thral dom)
chalk	al' ter	swarth y
talk	al der	war fare
stalk	al ways	war ble
dwarf	al so	ward en
wharf	cal dron	ward robe

war like	gaud y	a er o naut
war rior*	fau cet	mau so lē' um
warn ing	naugh ty	awe
al tar	haugh ty	hawk
bal sam	bau ble	brawl
with al'	caus tic	drawl
re ward	au tumn	spawn
re call	au gur	yawl
be fall	Au gust	yawn
in thrall	be daub'	aw' ful
in stall	de fraud	awn ing
ap pall	as sault	haw thorn
a thwart	a vaunt	law ful
a ward	ap plaud	law suit
talk' a tive	ap plause	taw dry
ald er man	de bauch	taw ny
sauce	aug ment	awk ward
gauze	au' di ble	tŏm' a hawk
laud	au di ence	straw ber ry
caught	au di tor	broad
taught	au thor ize	groat
naught	au to crat	a broad'
fraught	au spi ces	sought
aught	fraud u lent	thought
slaugh' ter	laud a ble	bought
daugh ter	nau ti lus	brought
au dit	au tŭm' nal	fought
plau dit	au then tic	wrought
au thor	ma raud er	nought
au burn	au thŏr' i ty	ought
lau rel	au tom a ton	be sought'
pau per	tau tol o gy	cough †
sau cer	au' di to ry	trough †

What words contain *oa* ? What contain or end in *ough* ?
* Pronounced war' vur.   † Pronounced kauf. trauf.

LESSON XCVII.

Words in which a and au have the sound of ĭ as in wad.

Fálse	false hood	quart er
swath	pal frey	quar rel
swaths	pal try	squan der
quash	pal sy	squad ron
wast	swal low	war rant
what	wal low	war ren
wal' let	wam pum	quad' ru ped
wal nut	fal ter	qual i ty
wan der	halt er	quan ti ty
wan ton	pal ter	quad ru ple
wad dle	psal ter	laud a num
swad dle	quad rant	sub al' tern
waf fle	quar ry	e qual'i ty

LESSON XCVIII.

Tar' dy.   does.   hear.   goes.   teach' er.   gone.

The Tardy Boy.

That boy is sliding on the ice. He has put his books on the stone.

He was on the way to school. His mother told him to make haste, lest he should be too late ; for it would soon be nine o'clock.   But he does not love his books. He is a lazy boy, and very fond of play.   The school-bell rings.   He hears it, and should go quickly, but he does not stop sliding.   He slides a long time.   At last, he goes to school.   He is very late.   The teacher tells him he has done wrong, and that he must stay after his schoolmates have gone home. This will make him sorry. His parents will be sorry too. For he will have to tell them of it. Good boys and girls will take care never to be tardy at school. Are *you* ever tardy?

LESSON XCIX.

Words in which a, au, and ea have the sound of $\frac{1}{a}$ as in bar.

Grȧnt	ba*l*m	g*u*ard .	brȧnch
chant	ca*l*m	aunt	stanch
pant	*p*sa*l*m	dȧunt	draft
ant	qua*l*m	haunt	draught
slant	pa*l*m	jaunt	laugh (lȧf)
snath	a*l*ms	flaunt	laugh′ ter
*w*rath	ca*l*f	gaunt	laugh′ a ble
a slant′	ha*l*f	vaunt *	hearth
ca tar*rh*	ca*l*ve	taunt	heart
a *gh*ast	ha*l*ve	saun′ ter	heart′ y
en chant	sa*l*ve	haunch	heart less
r*h*ū′ barb	*p*sa*l*m′ ist	launch	hart
ra*sp*′ ber ry	*p*sa*l*m′ o dy	lanch	aye

* Some pronounce vawnt.

LESSON C.

Words ending in et, it, ute, ait, oat, ot, ut, and at.

Mȧr′ ket	hab it	pōr trait .	horn et
bas ket	rab bit	ri ot	trump et
cas ket	orb it	pi lot	tip pet
gant let	cred it	wain scot	pup pet
gaunt let	lim it	waist coat	clar et ＼
scar let	sum mit	hȧr lot	tab ret
var let	vom it	ăb bot	gar ret
lan cet	her mit	tur bot	fer ret
gar net	mer it	fag got	lap pet
bŭck et	spir it	mag got	on set

buf fet	cul prit	big'ot	sun set
gib bet	viş it	im got	cloş et
dul cet	ex it	spig ot	gus set
hatch et	trans it	bal lot	rus set
latch et	min ute (it)	des pot	riv et
fresh et	in hab' it	car rot	vel vet
jack et	co hab it	par rot	ban quet
rack et	pro hib it	piv ot	mus ket
pack et	de·crep it	ā' pri cot	tab let
brack et	in her it	pa tri ot *	drib let
pick et	de poş it	id i ot	gob let
thick et	de mer it	pol y glot	mal let
crick et	cir' cuit (kit)	al i quot	pal let
tick et	bis cuit	gam' ut	bil let
wick et	con duit (dit)	chest nut	fil let
dock et	jeş' u it	car at	skil let
lock et	ben e fit	duc at	gul let

* Some, păt' ri ot.

What words end in *ute?* in *xit?* in *eit?* in *oat?* in *ut?* and in *et?*

LESSON CI.

Words ending in et, it, ite, ight, eit, ute, ip, ep, and op.

Sē' cret	sock et	cu bit
di et	blank et	bow sprit
qui et	trink et	pul pit
brace let	ring let	grăn ite
po et	cam let	res pite }
ca ret	ham let	res pit }
cru et	in let	def' i nite
su et	chap let ·	in fi nite
bul let	trip let	hyp o crite
pul let	corse let ·	req ui şite
pŏck et	helm et	per qui şite
rock et	ū nit	ex qui şite

ap po ṣite	run net	vī o let
op po ṣite	brisk et	bay o net
fā vor ite	front let	in tĕr′ pret
com pŏṣ′ ite	lin net	————
fort′ night	bon net	tū′ lip
for feit	son net	cow slip
sur feit	budg et	gŏs sip
coun′ ter feit	fidg et	tur nip ⎫
con trĭb′ute	al′ pha bet	tur nep ⎭
dis trib ute	ep i thet	pärs nep
at trib ute	am u let	bĭsh op
em′ met	riv u let	gal lop
plum met	cab i net	scal lop
com et	ep au let	shal lop
plan et	bar on et	scol lop
val et	cor o net	hȳs sop *
ten et	min a ret	de vĕl′ op
mag net	par a pet	en vel op ⎫
sig net	min u et	en vel ope ⎭

* Some pronounce hĭz′ zup.

What words end in *ight?* in *eit?* in *ute?* in *ep?*

LESSON CII.

Words ending in ire, yre, ipe, and ype.

Tīre	con spire	at tire	gripe
dire	as pire	săt′ ire	pipe
sire	re spire	vam pire	ripe
ire	in spire	em pire	tripe
quire	per spire	um pire	stripe
squire	ex pire	pis mire	wipe
wire	trans pire	quag mire	type
ac quīre′	de ṣire	lȳre	ăn′ ti type
re quire	re tire	pyre	prō to type
ad mire	en tire	snipe	stĕr′ e o type

What words end in *yre?* in *ype?*

LESSON CIII.

In the following words yte, ight, and eight are pronounced īte.

Mīte	in vite	fight	a light′
bite	re quite	light	de light
spite	in dict (īte)	blight	a right
rite	fī′ nite	flight	af fright
sprite	le vite	plight	twī′ light
trite	cŏn trite	slight	flight y
site	ex′ pe dite	night	might y
write	rec on dite	right	light en
ex cite′	sat el lite	bright	bright en
in cite	er u dite	fright	tight en
re cite	par a site	wright	fright en
in dite	ap pe tite	sight	sleight
po lite	pros e lyte	tight	{ height
u nite	coş mop′ o lite	wight	{ highth (hīt-th)
de spite	nīght′ in gale	knight	height′ en

What words end in, or contain *eight* ?

LESSON CIV.

In the following words yne and ign are pronounced īne.

Dīne	twine	re pine	sū per fine
fine	wine	sū′ pine	sign
shine	swine	cŏn′ cu bine	ĕn′ sign
vine	tine	crys tal line	as sign′
kine	sa line′	aq ui line	be nign
line	com bine	eg lan tine	con sign
mine	de fine	in ter line	con dign
nine	re fine	in fan tine	de sign
pine	con fine	por cu pine	re şign
spine	de cline	tur pen tine	ma lign
brine	re cline	val en tine	coun′ ter sign
shrine	in cline	brig an tine	as sign ēē′
thine	ca nine	an o dyne	con sign ee

What words end in, or contain *ign* ?

LESSON CV.
Les' son.   read.

The Girl who loved her Book.

Here is Jane once more.
She is coming from school,
  with a book in her hand.
She looks happy. Why is
  she happy?
She was a good girl at school.
She did not laugh nor play ;
but was attentive to her lessons, and careful to
obey her teacher. She was kind to her school
mates, and did to them as she would wish them
to do to her. They all love her much. The
teacher gave her the book, which she has in
her hand, because she behaved well. It is a
useful book, and she will love to read it. She
will carry it home. Her father and mother will
be glad to see it, and to find that Jane was a
good girl at school. Good boys and girls try
to behave well at school, because it makes their
parents happy. Do *you* do so?

LESSON CVI.
Words ending in īce, īse, ȳ, īgh, ȳe, īe, īed, and ī.

Dīce	thrice	vise	com ply
mice	price	pre cise'	im ply
rice	trice	con cise	re ply
vice	twice	păr' a dise	ap ply
lice	en tice'	wrȳ	sup ply
splice	ad vice	buy	Ju ly
slice	de vice	de fy'	de ny
ᵻce	rise	al ly	de cry

de scry	mod i fy	vil i fy	bye
es py	mol li fy	pet ri fy	eye
re ly	mor ti fy	viv i fy	dye
aw ry	nul li fy	cer ti fy	rye
beau' ti fy	oc cu py	liq ue fy	lye
cru' ci fy	os si fy	am pli fy	pie
glo ri fy	rar e fy	clas si fy	hie
no ti fy	rat i fy	mul ti ply	die
pu ri fy	rec ti fy	fals i fy	lie
pu tre fy	sanc ti fy	qual i fy	tie
stu pe fy	sat is fy	ĕd i fy	vie
de i fy	sig ni fy	in dem' ni fy	fie
dĭg ni fy	sim pli fy	per son i fy	pied
for ti fy	stul ti fy	i den ti fy	ma' gi
grat i fy	ter ri fy	di vers i fy	răb bi
just i fy	test i fy	hīgh	al' ka li
lull a by	ver i fy	nigh	gē ni i
mag ni fy	vers i fy	sigh	lit e ra' ti

What words end in *ise?* in *uy?* in *igh?* in *ye?* in *ie*, or contain *it?* and in *i?* What end in *efy?*

LESSON CVII.

In the following words ue at the end is silent.

Bŏg	ec' logue	vague	brōgue
cog	dem' a gogue	plague	vogue
flog	cat a logue	lēague	rogue
fog	ep i logue	cŏl' league	rogu' ish
hog	dec a logue	in trigue' *	rogu' er y
jog	syn a gogue	fa tigue *	pro rogue'
log	ped a gogue	ha răngue	dis em bogue'
frog	dī a logue	tongue (tŭng)	pro' logue

* Pronounced in trēg', fa tēg'.

LESSON CVIII

Words ending in ed, id, od, ad, and ud.

Hā' tred	rab' id	tor pid	stu pid
a ged	mor bid	sap id	dru id
na ked	tur bid	ar id	flu id
sa cred	flac cid	ac rid	fe tid
sto ried	ran cid	bed rid	squål id
tro phied	vis cid	flor id	pўr' a mid
gnårl ed	can did	hor rid	in va lid †
pål șied	splen did	tor rid	in trep' id
crăb bed	sor did	lan guid *	in sip id
wick ed	val id	liq uid	sal' ad
wretch ed	gel id	liv id	bal lad
kin dred	pal lid	viv id	meth od
hun dred	sol id	fer vid	syn od
stud ied	tim id	lū cid	trī ad
re nowned'	rap id	tu mid	pe' ri od
bĭg' ot ed	vap id	hu mid	mўr i ad
iș' o la ted	tep id	pu trid	o lym' pi ad
an ti qua ted	lim pid	lu rid	tal' mud

* Pronounced lăng' gwid. † Others pronounce in va lēēd'.

What words end in *ied*? in *ad*? in *od*? and in *ud*?

LESSON CIX.

Field.   dai' sy.   pret' ty.   ev' er y.

The Field Daisy.

I'm a pretty, little thing,
Always coming with the Spring.
In the meadows green I'm found,
Peeping just above the ground;
And my stalk is covered flat
With a white and yellow hat.

Little lady, when you pass
Lightly o'er the tender grass,
Skip about, but do not tread
On my meek and lowly head;
For I always seem to say,
" Chilly Winter 's gone away."

Where is God?

In the sun, the moon, the sky;
On the mountain, wild and high;
In the thunder, in the rain,
In the grove, the wood, the plain;
In the little birds that sing;
God is seen in every thing.

LESSON CX.

Words in which ear, eer, ere, ire, and ier have the sound of ēre.

Clēar	year	jeer
dear	gear	leer
fear	beard*	sneer
hear	be smear'	peer
shear	en dear'	seer
blear	ap pear'	queer
ear	up rear'	steer
smear	ar rear'	veer
near	dis ap pear'	ve neer'
spear	ap pear' ance	ca reer
rear	beer	mount ain eer'
drear	deer	en gi neer
sear	cheer	dom i neer
tear	sheer	vol un teer

son net eer	sin cere'	gla cier *
gaz et teer	ad here	cash ier
pam phlet eer	co here	der nier
fu şil eer	aus tere	fin an cier'
mu ti neer	re vere	brig a dier
pi o neer	se vere	gren a dier
o ver seer	per se vere'	cav a lier
pri va teer	hem'i sphere	çhev a lier
mu let eer	at mos phere	çhan de lier
auc tion eer	shire *	gon do lier
char i ot eer'	bier	can non ier
mere	tier	buc a nier
sere	pier	cuir as sier
sphere	fron tier'	(kwĕr as seer)

* Some pronounce shīre, glā shēr'.

What words end in *ire* and *ier?*

LESSON CXI.

Words in which ea, ee, e, ei, ie, and i, have the sound of ē as in here.

Bēad	creed	se cede	teat
lead	freed	con cede	wheat
plead	seed	im pede	de feat'
mead	weed	in ter cede'	re peat
knead	steed	su per sede	en treat
read	suc ceed'	eat	re treat
deed	pro ceed	beat	beet
feed	ex ceed	feat	feet
heed	in deed	cheat	sheet
bleed	mis deed	bleat	fleet
meed	a greed	heat	sleet
need	cede	meat	meet
speed	ac cede'	neat	greet
reed	re cede	peat	street
breed	pre cede	treat	sweet

dis creet'	beak	freak	creek *
mete	leak	screak	greek
re plete'	bleak	squeak	seek
com plete	sneak	weak	week
se crete	peak	cheek	eke
cŏn' crete	speak	leek	shriek
ob' so lete	streak	sleek	pique (pēk)
de ceit'	tweak	meek	ob lique't
con ceit	wreak	reek	an tique
re ceipt	creak	peek	u nique

* Others pronounce krĭk, † ob līke.

What words end in *ead?* in *sede?* in *ete?* in *eit* and *eipt?* in *eke?* in *iek* and *ique?*

LESSON CXII.

Words in which ea, ee, ei, e, i, ie, and eo have the sound of ē
as in here.

Dēal	keel	stream' er	yean
heal	peel	squeam ish	sheen
meal	reel	deem	keen
peal	kneel	seem	spleen
seal	steel	teem	screen ⎫
steal	gen teel'	re deem'	skreen ⎬
veal	teil	es teem	green
squeal	ceil	theme	seen
weal	beam	ex treme'	teen
zeal	gleam	su preme	queen
con ceal'	ream	blas pheme	ween
con geal	scream	bean	ca reen'
ap peal	cream	dean	tu reen
re peal	dream	lean	be tween
re veal	stream	clean	pis ta reen'
eel	seam	glean	scene
feel	team	mean	ob scene'
heel	steam	wean	se rene

ter rene	ma rine	mien	keep
con vene	rou tine*	man da rin'	deep
găn' grene	mag a zine'	weep	reap
con tra vene'	quar an tine	steep	heap
su per vene	ma çhi' nist	sweep	leap
in ter vene	ma çhin' er y	sleep	cheap
ra vine'	lien	sheep	neap
ma çhine	sein)	peep	stee' ple
ton tine	seine) .	creep	peo ple

What words end in *eil*? in *ame*? in *ine*? in *ien*? in *ein*? and in *in*?
What word contains *eo*?   * *ou*, as *o* in move.

LESSON CXIII.

Words in which ea, ee, ie, and ei, have the sound of ē as in
here.

Bēach	priest	grief	re lieve
bleach	teeth	chief	re prieve
each	wreath	lief	re trieve
breach	heath	thief	griev' ous
preach	sheath	fief	griev ance
peach	seethe	be lief'	con ceive'
teach	wreath	re lief	de ceive
im peach'	sheathe	sleeve	per ceive
beech	breathe	peev' ish	re ceive
leech	be neath'	cleave	ei' ther
speech	be queath	heave	nei ther
breech*	wreaths	leave	leiṣ ure *
screech	sheaths	weave	seiz ure
be seech'	beef	be reave'	in vei' gle
beast	reef	thieve	o bei sance
least	sheaf	grieve	field
yeast	leaf	ag grieve'	shield
east	deaf*	a chieve	wield
feast	brief	be lieve	yield

* Some pronounce brĭch, dĕf, lĕzh ur.

un wield' y	siege	ea' şy	sieve (sĭv)
fiend	be siege'	bea ver	mĭs' chief (chĭf)
liege	leash	wea ry	hand' ker chief

What words end in *iest*? in *eaf*? in *eive*? What others contain *ei*?

LESSON CXIV.

Words ending in ea, ay, ey, ie, i, e, and ee.

Pēa	mot ley	bēē	ven dee
lea	lam prey	fee	mort ga gee'
flea	chim ney	knee	ob li gee
tea	guín ea	thee	ref u gee
plea	clāy ey	lee	deb au çhee
sea	prair ie	flee	ap pel lee
yea *	spe cie †	glee	ref er ee
bo hea'	câu şey	free	dis a gree
key	pár ley	tree	prom i see
quay (kē)	bar ley	three	o ver see
lăck' ey	pars ley	see	leg a tee
jock ey	ban dĭt' ti	lĕv' ee	guar an tee
tur key	com mit tee	cof fee	ab sen tee
med ley	sper ma cē' ti	gran dēē'	pat en tee
al ley	ăc' me	a gree	dev o tee
gal ley	sim' i le	de gree	rep ar tee
val ley	hy per' bo le	gran tee	wâr ran tee
vol ley	e pit o me	trus tee	jū' bi lee
pŭl ley	ex tem po re	set tee	pĕd i gree
hăck ney	ca tas tro phe	de cree	Phar i see
kid ney	a pos tro phe	ra zee	Sad du cee

* Some pronounce yā.   † Pronounced spē' shy.

What words end in *ea*? in *ey*? in *ie*? and in *i*?

LESSON CXV.

Words in which ea, ee, ie, ei, e, and i, in monosyllables and the last syllables, have the sound of ē as in here.

| Plēaşe | teaşe | diş eaşe |
| ease | ap pease' | cheese |

these	ab o rig´ i neş *	peace
breeze	an tip´ o deş †	fleece
wheeze	cease	geese
freeze	lease	niece
squeeze	crease	piece
frieze	grease -	ca price´
seize	de crease´	po lice
leeş	in crease	va lise
se´ri eş	re lease	pe lisse
ŏb´ se quieş	de cease	frŏnt´ is piece

* Pronounced ab o rĭj´ e nēz. † Some pronounce an´ tĕ pōdz.

What words end in *ieze*? in *eize*? *iece*? *ice*? and *ise*?

LESSON CXVI.

Nev´ er.   par tak´ er.   when.

Proverbs ; or short, wise sayings.

Rolling the *little* snowball makes the *great* one.

An angry man never wants trouble.

Nothing can need a lie.

The partaker is as bad as the thief.

A boy is known by the company that he keeps.

Much would have more, and lost all.

Tardy at school, tardy through life.

When *one* will not quarrel, *two* cannot.

Be slow to speak of the faults of others.

A little wrong done to *another*, is a great wrong to *one's self.*

Empty things sound the loudest.

One lie makes another.

It is good to *begin* well ; it is better to *end* well.

LESSON CXVII.
Words of three syllables, accented on the first.

Dī´a dem	wa ri ness	pen te cost
di a gram	pu gi list	pov er ty
do na tive	su i cide	rem e dy
cu ra tive	ru bi cund	tap es try
lu cra tive	sto i cişm	trav es ty
he bra işm	lone li ness	un der ling
he bra ist	boun ti ful	in tel lect
di a lect	e go tişm	sol e cişm
hy a cinth	e go tist	sym me try
dy nas ty	hu mo rist	mag ne tişm
ri val ry	eu lo gy	maj es ty
fe al ty	pro to col	mod es ty
rheu ma tişm	lŭck i ly	hon es ty
a the işm	guar an ty	mul ber ry
a the ist	leth ar gy	hap pi ness
du el list }	am nes ty	hom i ly
du el ist }	bod i ly	man i fest
pu ber ty	as ter isk	man i fold
cru el ty	com e dy	man li ness
like li hood	el e gy	mul·ti form
live li hood	en e my	prod i gy
hast i ly	en er gy	pär ti tive
fu gi tive	lib er ty	har di hood
pu ni tive	ob e lisk	bar ba rişm
u ni form	emp ti ness	tar di ness
u ni corn	pan the işm	craft i ly
ho li ness	pan the ist	mount e bank

LESSON CXVIII.
Words of three syllables, accented on the first.

Făm´ i ly	aq ue duct	nov el ty
an ces try	nov el ist	tal is man

crit i cişm	ret i cule	croc o dile
cap ri corn	rid i cule	par ox yşm
dif fi cult	sat ir ist	ex or cişm
ef fi gy	mat ri cide	ret ro spect
trans i tive	frat ri cide	mel o dy
poş i tive	par ri cide	meth od işm
gen i tive	hom i cide	meth od ist
sub stan tive	per fi dy	col lo quy
ep i gram	des ti ny	ob lo quy
hand i craft	ad jec tive	al co hol
hand i work	sen si tive	rhap so dy
lab y rinth	ab so lute	mon o tone
min is try	col o ny	pan to mime
rep ri mand	col o nist	caş u ist
rud di ness	big ot ry	lit ur gy
sub si dy	cus to dy	ex ple tive
mys ti cişm	des pot işm	oc u list
fan ci ful	her o işm	cal um ny
mer ci ful	mon o dy	in dus try
pit i ful	pan o ply	in ju ry
plen ti ful	par o dy	per ju ry
scep ti cişm ⎫	pros o dy	cir cum spect
skep ti cişm ⎭	syl lo gişm	man u script
ves ti bule	cam o mile	man u mit

LESSON CXIX.

Words of two and three syllables, accented on the first.

Gár' land	thou şand	al mond	em e rald
hŏl land	lē gend	dī' a mond	scaf' fold
er rand	prĕb end	gĕr' und	scab bard
gor mand	div' i dend	joc und	stand ard
huş band	rev e rend	her ald	hag gard
huş' band ry	stī' pend	her' ald ry	nig gard
vī' end	sĕc ond	rib ald ry	slug gard

or chard	haz ard	way ward	short est
tank ard	liz ard	hăl berd	long est
drunk ard	wiz ard	shep herd	swift est
spike nard	giz zard	pot sherd	lárg est
leop ard	buz zard	reo ord	har vest
jeop ard	dō tard	cup board	pā pist
cus tard	home ward	bal last	lo cust
mus tard	stew ard	mod est	bold est
wind ward	steel yard ·	hon est	kind est
back ward	fro ward	tem pest	ĭn' ter est
vine yard	to ward	for est	am e thyst

What words end in *ond*? in *und*? in *old*? and in *erd*?

LESSON CXX.

Words in which ea, ai, ay, ie, and ei, have the sound of ĕ as in red.

Brĕad	breast	earn est	stead fast
dead	cleanse	earth en	bed stead
dread	earl	feath er	stealth y
head	pearl	leath er	threat en
tread	hearse	leath ern	weap on
lead	learn	hogs head	weath er
read	earn	heav y	zeal ous
spread	yearn	lead en	jeal ous
stead	realm	dead en	a breast'
thread	dealt	dead ly	a head
breadth	meant	mead ow	be head
breath	dreamt	leav en	be spread
death	sweat	heav en	be stead
dearth	threat	peas ant	in stead
earth	search	pheas ant	re search
health	brĕak' fast	pleas ant	re hearse
stealth	clean ly	read y	re hears' al
wealth	ear ly	stead y	ăl read y

en deav or	treach er ous	saith	says (sĕz)
read′ i ly	treach er y	a gain′	friend
read i ness	said	a gainst	heif′ er

What words contain ai, ay, ie, and ei?

LESSON CXXI.

Words ending in nce and nse.

Chȧnce	dis pense	mince
dance	in tense	prince
lance	ex pense	since
glance	sus pense	quince
prance	in cense	wince
trance	non′ sense	rinse
mis chance′	lī censé	e vince′
per chance	frank ĭn′ cense*	con vince
en hance	fence	prov′ ince
a skance	hence	sconce
en trance	thence	ounce
ad vance	whence	bounce
ro mănce	pence	flounce
fi nance	com mence′	pounce
ex panse	de fence ⎫	trounce
dense	de fense ⎬	de nounce′
sense	of fence ⎪	re nounce
tense	of fense ⎭	an nounce
con dense′	pre tence ⎫	pro nounce
im mense	pre tense ⎭	dŭnce

* Others, frănk′ in cense.

What words end in anse? in inse? in once? and unce?

LESSON CXXII.

Words ending in rce and rse.

Fȧrce	fïerce *	scărce	verse
parse	pierce *	co ĕrce′	terse
sparse	tïerce *	a merce	hearse

* Some pronounce fĕrs, pĕrs, tĕrs.

re hearse´	re verse	trav erse	di vorce´
curse	in verse	dī verse	source
nurse	per verse	u´ ni verse	re source´
purse	trans verse	hŏrse	coarse
con verse´	in ter sperse´	corse	hoarse
as perse	dis burse´	re morse´	course
dis perse	re im burse´	en dorse }	re course´
im merse	com´ merce	in dorse }	dis course
a verse _	ad verse	fōrce	cŏn´ course

What words end in *ree* ?

LESSON CXXIII.

Words ending in s, ss, sse, and sce.

Găs	dress	re press
a las´	stress	im press
sas´ sa fras _	press	com press
áss	chess	op press
bass	guess	dis tress
lass	ac cess´	ex press
class ..	suc cess	as sess
glass	re cess	pos sess
mass	con fess	ab´ scess
pass	pro fess	in gress
brass	ex cess	pre pos sess´
grass	un less	nev er the less´
a mass´	ca ress	fi nesse´
re pass	ad dress	ac qui esce´
sur pass	re dress	co a lesce
mo răss	e gress	ef fer vesce
less	ag gress	bŏss
bless	di gress	cross
tress	trans gress	loss
mess	de press	gloss

moss	a cross'	fuss
dross	em boss	truss
toss	ma tross	dis cuss'

What words end in *as*? What in *sse*? in *esce*? What monosyllables end in single *s*? See Rule IV. for spelling, page 161.

LESSON CXXIV.

Blue.   glad' den.

God made all things.

God made the sky so bright and
    blue,
  God made the grass so green ;
He made the flowers that smell
    so sweet,
  In pretty colors seen.

God made the little birds to fly ;
  How sweetly they have sung ;
And though they soar so very high,
  They wont forget their young.

God made the cow to give us milk,
  The horse for us to use ;
I'll treat them kindly for his sake,
  Nor dare his gifts abuse.

God made the sun that shines so bright,
  And gladdens all I see,
It comes to give us heat and light ;
  How thankful I should be.

God made the moon and stars on high,
  To rule the darksome night ;
How bright they shine in yonder sky,
  To cheer us with their light.

LESSON CXXV.

Words ending in ss, s, se, and ce.

Hïss	pa ren the sis	ed i fice
kiss	hy poth e sis	or i fice
bliss	a nal y sis	av a rice
miss	pa ral y sis	den ti frice
a miss′	a man u en′ sis	lic o rice
re miss	nō′ tice (tĭs)	ȧr mis tice
dis miss	poul tice	ar ti fice
a byss	jäun dice	ac cŏm′ plice
ī′ ris	ŏf fice	ap pren tice
ba sis	mal ice	mor′ tise
cri sis	sur plice	prom ise
gra tis	cor nice	fran chise
clăs sis	cop pice	prac tice
der vis	sol stice	trēat ise
ax is	just ice	prĕf ace
em′ pha sis	lat tice	sur face
syn the sis	crev ice	pal ace
gen e sis	nov ice	neck lace
o ā′ sis	serv ice	sol ace
pro bŏs cis	let tuce (tĭs)	men ace
el lip sis	tor toise	pin nace
sy nop sis	cow′ ard ice	fur nace
me trop′ o lis	prĕj u dice	ter race
an tith e sis	ben e fice	pur chase

What words end in *yss?* in *uce?* in *oise?* in *ise?* in *ace?*

LESSON CXXVI.

Words ending in s, ss, and se,

Căn′ vas	cŏp′ per as	tres pass
at las	er y sip′ e las	can vass
bï as	wind′ lass	har ass

cut lass	rūth less	cĭr cus
căr cass	cy press	sŭr plus
em băr′ rass	jew ess	isth mus
ab′ bess	prow ess	cen sus
prin cess	heed less	in′ cu bus
reck less	peer less	ex o dus
bur gess	child less	im pe tus
em press	seam stress	gē ni us
wit ness	lăr gess	ra di us
con gress *	har ness	pros pĕc′ tus
prog ress	dī′ o cese ⎫	co los sus
ac tress	di o cess ⎭	Le vit′ i cus
for tress	re′ bus	as par a gus
mis tress	fo cus	ap pa rā′ tus
mat tress ⎫	mu cus	pŭr′ pose
mat ress ⎭	ge nus	por poise ⎫
but tress	vi rus	por pess ⎭

* Pronounced kŏng′ gres.

What words end in ess? in oss? in oise?

LESSON CXXVII.

Words in which oo, and accented o have the sound of o as in move.

Rood	booth	hoof	ooze
brood	smooth	woof	cool
mood	soothe	broom	loon
food	tooth	groom	swoon
moor	scoop	loom	roost
boor	stoop	room	school
poor	whoop	goose	groove
moot	swoop	loose	boo′ by
boot	troop	moose	boot y
shoot	roof	noose	bo som
hoot	proof	choose	bride groom

pan ta loon'	dra goon	rac coon	re move
for sooth'	fes toon	sa loon	re prove
a loof	har poon	pol troon	im prove
bab oon	lam poon	mon soon	ap prove
bal loon	la goon	be hoof	dis prove
bas soon	pla toon	be hoove }	en tomb
buf foon	pon toon	be hove. }	hĕc' a tomb

What word ends in *ze*? In which words does single *o* sound as in move?

LESSON CXXVIII.

Words in which ou, oeu, oo, oe, and the o in monosyllables and accented syllables, have the sound of o as in move.

Group	ac cou tre }	too
croup	ac cou ter }	a do'
soup	ma nœu vre }	*w*ho
sou	ma neu ver }	*w*hóse
tour	rĕn' dez vouş	*w*hom
tour' ist	tour na ment	*w*ho' so ev er
car touch'	t*w*o	cŭck' oo
sur tout	tomb	tat too'
un couth	coo	shoe
con tour	woo	ca noe'

What words end in *ous*? in *oo*? in *oe*?

LESSON CXXIX.

Words in which ieu, ue, ew, iew, ou, ewe, and eau are found.

Lieu (lū)	blue	ven due	văl ue
pŭr' lieu	glue	im brue	con strue
lieu ten' ant	rue	ac crue	is sue *
a dieu' (dū)	true	en sue	tis sue *
cue (kū)	sue	pur sue	stat ue
due	im bue'	rĕs' cue	vĭr tue
hue	sub due	ăr gue	rĕş' i due
flue	in due	ā gue	av e nue

rev e nue	clew ⎫	stew ,	neph ew
ret i nue	clue ⎭	strew	pur view
con tin' ue	new	grew	cur few
im promp tu	threw	*k*new	sin ew
dew	flew	yew	re new'
few	brew	ewe (yū)	re view
hew	crew	yoū	ĭn' ter view
chew	screw	youth	beaū' ty
drew	shrew	through	beau' ti ful
view	slew	mĭl' dew	beau te ous

What words end in, or contain *ieu?* What end in *u?* in *ewe?* in *ough?* in *iew?* What contain *eau?*

LESSON CXXX,

Fa' ble.   oft' en.   which.   thirst.   af' ter.

The Fable of the Crow and the Jug.

[A fable is a short story, to teach the truth in a pleasing way. It often supposes things to happen which never did happen—not to deceive us, but to instruct and amuse. You will see this in the following fable.]

A crow that was dry, strove to quench her thirst in a jug which had some water in it. But the neck of the jug was so long and narrow, that the poor bird could not get her head in. "Well," said she, "I think I can tell what to do with you yet. Come, let me see; I will fill you partly with stones, and then, I dare say, the water will rise to the top, do what you can to prevent it." So the crow went to work, as you see in the picture. She dropped in one stone after another; and in a short time the water rose so high, that she had as much of it as she pleased.

This fable teaches us, that by *planning* and *persevering*, we may often do what we think, at first, cannot be done.

"*I cannot*," never did any thing. "*I will try*," has done wonders.

LESSON CXXXI.

Words in which ure, our, eur, ewer, ew, eu, ude, eud, and ewd are found.

Pūre	ma ture	min i a ture
lure	your	tem per a ture
sure (shūr)	ĕp′ i cūre	lit er a ture
in sure′	sī ne cure	jū di ca ture
as sure	o ver ture	hew′ er
se cure	por trai ture	ew er
pro cure	pre ma ture	skew er
ob scure	līg a ture	brew er
en dure	sig na ture	sew er
ab jure	cur va ture	pew ter
al lure	for feit ure	neu ter
de mure	fur ni ture	crūde
im mure	ap er ture	prude
ma nure	am a teūr′	rude
in ure	con nois seur	pre′ lude
ad jure	căr′ i ca ture	pre clude′

se clude   lon gi tude   al ti tude
e lude   lat i tude   serv i tude
in clude   sol i tude   prompt i tude
con clude   am pli tude   quī e tude
ex clude   mag ni tude   dis qui' e tude
de lude   tur pi tude   si mil i tude
al lude   las si tude   in fin i tude
ob trude   rec ti tude   de crep i tude
in trude   grat i tude   vi cis si tude
pro trude   at ti tude   be at i tude
ex ude   mul ti tude   feûd
in' ter lude apt i tude   lewd
hab i tude   for ti tude   shrewd

What words end in *our?* in *eur?* in *eud?* in *ewd?* in *etude?*

LESSON CXXXII.
Words ending in a.

Sō' fa   a re a   form u la
ga la   hy e na   stam i na
dra ma   au ro ra   al ge bra
e ra   er ra ta   gen e ra
quo ta   i o ta   op e ra
so da   di plo ma   ret i na
stra ta   sa li va   ef flū' vi a
ze bra   um brel la   mal a rí a
vil la   di lem ma   pen in su la
stig ma   e nig ma   a nath e ma
dog ma   ho san na   in sig ni a
asth ma   pi az za   a poc ry pha
com ma   mi as ma   phe nom e na
vis ta   ve ran da   in flu en' za
stan za   cū' po la   pan o ra ma
man na   ma ni a   hy dro phō' bi a
i dē' a   scrŏf u la   en cy clo pe' di a

LESSON CXXXIII.

Words of four and five syllables, accented variously.

Re stō' ra tive	ge om e try	fig' u ra tive
ac cu şa tive	e van gel ist	im i ta tive
pro vo ca tive	im pov er ish	caş u al ty
in tu i tive	fa nat i cişm	pres by ter y
le vi a than	in fan ti cide	em i nent ly
en thu şi aşm	a nal o gy	dif fi cul ty
en thu şi ast	a nat o my	ap o plex y
de rŏg a tive	an tag o nist	caş u is try
con serv a tive	a pol o gist	con tu me ly
im per a tive	a ris to crat	pol y the işm
pre rog a tive	as trol o gy	af fi dā' vit
in dic a tive	a pol o gy	pan e gȳr ist
su per la tive	as tron o my	mul ti pli cand'
de fin i tive	e con o my	com mū' ni ca tive
in fin i tive	ge ol o gy	vi tu pe ra tive
in quiş i tive	mo nop o ly	de mo ni' a cal
re trib u tive	the ol o gy	in ter rŏg a tive
dis trib u tive	my thol o gy	rep re şent a tive
di min u tive	phi lol o gy	or ni thol o gy
con sec u tive	tau tol o gy	gen e al o gy
an tip a thy	phre nol o gy	min e ral o gy
a nom a ly	zo ol o gy	trig o nom e try
po lyg a my	mis an thro py	et y mol o gy
i dol a try	dox ol o gy	phyş i ol o gy
a cad e my	ven tril o quişm	phra şe ol o gy

LESSON CXXXIV.

In the following words ise and ice have the sound of īze.

Rīse	ex cise'	sur mise
guise	de mise	de spise
wise	pre mise	a rise

em prise

com prise

ap prise

chas tise

ad vise

de vise

re vise

dis guise

crĭt′ i cise

cĭr cum cise

ĕx er cise

mer chan dise

com pro mise

en ter prise

ex or cise

mod ′ern ize

sym bol ize

ad ver tise′

su per vise

suf fice′

săc′ ri fice

prīze

size

as size′

ap prize

bap tize

ē′ qual ize

neu tral ize

re al ize

le gal ize

bru tal ize

i dol ize

hu man ize

scru ti nize

the o rize

mĕth od ize

gor man dize

ag gran dize

rec og nize)
rec og nise }

col o nize

can on ize

pat ron ize

jour nal ize

pul ver ize

tem po rize

ser′mon ize

sym pa thize

scan dal ize

sig nal ize

mor al ize

tan ta lize

crys tal lize)
crys tal ize }

fer til ize

civ il ize

tyr an nize

sub si dize

ag o nize

or gan ize

par a lyze)
par a lize }

sol em nize

sat ir ize

stig ma tize

mag net ize

dog ma tize

an a lyze

hár mo nize

i tăl′ i cize

e pit o mize

ex tem po rize

a pol o gize

a pos tro phize

phi los o phize

im mor tal ize

e van gel ize

mo nop o lize

e con o mize

a pos ta tize

so lil o quize

nat′ u ral ize

gen er al ize

sec u lar ize

sys tem a tize

ma tē′ ri al ize

par tĭc u lar ize

a nath e ma tize

spir′ it u al ize

rev o lū′ tion ize

What words end in *ise?* in *yze?*

He who is behind-hand, makes work for himself, and trouble for others.

Virtue is the only true nobility.

LESSON CXXXV.

Words ending in ant and ent, of two syllables, accented on the first.

Va'cant	dē cent	stag nant	urg ent
pa geant	re cent	rem nant	tal ent
gi ant	tri dent	flip pant	clem ent
pli ant	pru dent	ar rant	com ment
claim ant	stu dent	cur rant	pen dent
poign ant	a gent	mer chant	vest ment
fla grant	re gent	pen dant	ser pent
ty rant	co gent	pleas ant	cur rent
tru ant	cli ent	peas ant	ab sent
fra grant	si lent	pheas ant	pat ent
va grant	pave ment	dis tant	pres ent
pĕd ant	oint ment	in stant	ad vent
ver dant	mo ment	con stant	con vent
ser geant*	la tent	ex tant	fer vent
in fant	po tent	sex tant	sol vent
gal lant	flu ent	serv ant	ar dent
dor mant	lăm bent	tan gent	gar ment
ten ant	cres cent	pun gent	parch ment

* Others pronounce sar' jent.

LESSON CXXXVI.

Words ending in ant and ent, of three syllables, accented on the second.

Com pli'ant	de fend ant	in dul gent
as sail ant	at tend ant	ef ful gent
com plain ant	re cum bent	re ful gent
ac count ant	in cum bent	as trin gent
pur su ant	qui es cent	con tin gent
as cĕnd ant	tran scend ent	in sur gent
de scend ant	re splen dent	in clem ent

im port ant	in ces sant	ad jā cent
as sist ant	re luct ant	com pla cent
ob serv ant	re pent ant	im pru dent
a bund ant	a but ment	de port ment
re dund ant	con cur rent	de po nent
ac cord ant	re spond ent	com po nent
con cord ant	con ver gent	op po nent
dis cord ant	con sist ent	ad he rent
in form ant	in sol vent	in he rent
in dig nant	de lin quent	co he rent
ma lig nant	de pend ent	en roll ment
re pug nant	ab hor rent	a part ment

LESSON CXXXVII.
Words ending in ent and ant, of three syllables, accented on the first.

Lē′ni ent	dil i gent	ar ro gant
o ri ent	prev a lent	ad a mant
vi o lent	pest i lent	ad ju tant
ve he ment	ex cel lent	com bat ant
ru di ment	in do lent	con ver sant
nu tri ment	in so lent	com plai sant
in no cent	tur bu lent	dis pu tant
ac ci dent	op u lent	men di cant
in ci dent	cor pu lent	sup pli cant
dif fi dent	vir u lent	rec re ant
con fi dent	flat u lent	mis cre ant
res i dent	lig a ment	ter ma gant
pres i dent	firm a ment	sup pli ant
ev i dent	or na ment	dis so nant
prov i dent	sac ra ment	pet u lant
im pu dent	con fi dant	stim u lant
in di gent	el e gant	con so nant
neg li gent	el e phant	oc cu pant

ig no rant	bat tle ment	im mi nent
em i grant	ten e ment	lin i ment
mil i tant	chas tiṣe ment	prom i nent
viṣ it ant	sed i ment	con ti nent
prot est ant	con di ment	per ti nent
rel e vant	al i ment	ab sti nent
rā di ant	com pli ment	rev er ent
par lia ment	mer ri ment	com pe tent
ar ma ment	det ri ment	pen i tent
ar gu ment	sen ti ment	eṣ cu lent
test a ment	doc u ment	im po tent
el e ment	mon u ment	af flu ent
im ple ment	in stru ment	sub se quent
com ple ment	per ma nent	con se quent
sup ple ment	em i nent	el o quent

LESSON CXXXVIII.

Words ending in ent and ant, of four and five syllables, accented variously.

o bē′ di ent	com mū ni cant	e mol u ment
ex pe di ent	lux u ri ant	om nip o tent
in gre di ent	sig nif i cant	con stit u ent
a pe ri ent	ex trav a gant	in tel li gent
be nĕf i cent	pre pond er ant	con va les′ cent
mag nif i cent	in tol er ant	in de pend ent
mu nif i cent	i tin er ant	cor re spond ent
co in ci dent	in hab i tant	om ni preṣ ent
per cip i ent	con com i tant	in ter mit tent
re cip i ent	be nev o lent	in ad vert ent
sub serv i ent	pre dic a ment	an te cē dent
in cip i ent	ad ver tiṣe ment	lin′ e a ment
e quiv a lent	im ped i ment	tem per a ment
ma lev o lent	ex per i ment	su per in tend′ ent

LESSON CXXXIX.
Fall' en.   e' qual.

The vain Jackdaw.

A foolish jackdaw once picked up some feathers which had fallen from a peacock ; and, putting them on, made himself as fine as he could. Becoming very vain, he began to slight the company of other jackdaws. He joined a flock of beautiful peacocks, and thought himself as fine as the best of them. They knew who he was, and resolved to get rid of him. So they tore the borrowed plumes from his back, and pecked him out of their company. He then tried to get back among his old friends, the jackdaws. These, also, resenting his former pride, refused to receive him; while one of the most honest among them thus addressed him. "If you had been contented to remain a jackdaw, you would have avoided this double disgrace."

We learn from this, never to set ourselves up above our equals, nor to pretend to be what we are not.

LESSON CXL.

In the following words, ur, er, and ir, have nearly the same sound.

Bŭr	her	perch	third
cur	de. ter'	herd	fir
slur	de fer	herb	sir
fur	pre fer	verb	stir
blur	re fer	serf	first
spur	in fer	serve	whirl
pŭrr }	con fer	swerve	whir
pur }	trans fer	nerve	sir' up
oc cur'	a ver	were	stir rup
re cur	in ter	pre serve'	dirge
con cur	jerk	re serve	merge
in cur	clerk	de serve	verge
de mur	yerk	su perb	e merge'
ab surd	berth	mer' maid	di verge
sul' phur	sperm	ster ling	con verge
mur mur	term	di vers	urge
pur port	germ	ice berg	purge
err	erst	bird	surge

LESSON CXLI.

In the following words, ur, er, or, ir, and yr, have nearly the same sound.

Hŭrt	re turn'	cis tern
spurt	u surp	pat tern
lurk	fern	slat tern
urn	stern	bit tern
burn	con cern'	cav ern
churn	dis cern	tav ern
spurn	mod' ern	north ern
turn	lan tern	west ern

ēast ern	di vert	chirp
pos tern	de ṣert	twirl
a corn	deṣ ṣert	birth
stŭb born	a lert	mirth
wert	ō′ vert	birch
pert	dĕṣ ert	thirst
ex pert′	fil bert	squirm
in sert	con′ tro vert	firm
as sert	an i mad vert′	af firm′
a vert	dirt	in firm
sub vert	shirt	con firm
ad vert	flirt	sir′ loin
in ert	squirt	skirm ish
re vert	quirk	cir′ cum stance
con vert	irk	cir cum vĕnt′
con cert	dirk	myrrh (mĕr)

What words end in *ern?* in *yrrh?*

LESSON CXLII.
Words ending in dge and ge.

Bădge	budge	lodg ment
edge	judge	a bridg′ ment
hedge	drudge	ac *knowl′* edg ment
ledge	grudge	cot′ tage
pledge	trudge	cab bage
sledge	*knowl*′edge	ad age
fledge	selv edge	band age
dredge	por ridge	bond age
sedge	căr tridge	cord age
wedge	a brĭdge′	bag gage
ridge	dis lodge	lug gage
bridge	ac *knowl′* edge	mort gage
dodge	fore *knowl* edge	car riage
̶ ̶ ̶ge	judg′ ment	mar riage

pil lage	im age	spin age
til lage	pack age	stop page
vil lage	rum mage	man age
dam age	hom age	suf frage

Plŭ' mage	sav age	dis par age
out rage	um brage	ad van tage
u şage	lan guage *	ar rear age
do tage	salv age	cŏl' lege
post age	lin' e age	al lege' ⎱
port age	vas sal age	al ledge ⎰
voy age	pil grim age	priv' i lege
car nage	hem or rhage	sac ri lege
såu sage	pat ron age	ves' tige
fŏr age	per son age	del uge
viş age	eq ui page	ref uge
mes sage	av er age	sub' ter fuge
vint age	bev er age	en gāge'
host age	her mi tage	as suage
pot age	her i tage	pre sage
rav age	ap pend' age	o blige †

* Pronounced lăng' gwaj.　† Some pronounce o blēj'.

Which word ends in *edge?* What in *iage?* in *ige?*

LESSON CXLIII.

Words ending in am, em, egm, im, ym, ime, and om.

Măd' am	sā chem	min' im
bed lam	po em	max im
buck ram	i tem	vic tim
ep' i gram	străt' a gem	pil grim
an them	rē qui em	thum mim
em blem	the o rem	ū rim
prob lem	phlĕgm	sĕr' a phim
sys tem	ap' o thegm	cher u bim

san he drim	wiş dom	bux om
in ter im	faţh om	ran som
syn o nym	ven om	cus tom
mar i time	blos som	frēē dom
ver bā′ tim	at om	be şom
kĭng′ dom	bot tom	ac cŭs′ tom
sel dom	phan tom	id′ i om
ran dom	symp tom	mår tyr dom

What words end in *am*? in *egm*?, in *ym*? in *ime*?

LESSON CXLIV.

Words ending in um, ume, and ome.

Fō′ rum	mu şe um	e qui lib′ ri um
quo rum	as y lum	lōne′ some
stra tum	de co rum	*w*hole some
ăl um	po ma tum	tire some
vel lum	mo mĕn tum	noi some
nos trum	en cō′ mi um	wea′ ri some
ros trum	em po ri um	blithe′ some
vol ume	op pro bi um	fŭl some
mē′ di um	pal l̃a di um	wel come
o di um	gym na şi um	in come
o pi um	com pĕnd i um	glad some
pre mi um	mil len ni um	hand some
pĕnd u lum	de lir i um	frol′ ic some ⎫
vac u um	mem o ran′ dum	frol ick some ⎬
ly cē′ um	in ter reg num	cum ber some ⎭

THE BUTTERFLY.

The Butterfly, an idle thing,
Nor honey makes, nor yet can sing,
  Like to the bee and bird;
Nor does it, like the prudent ant,
Lay up the grain for times of want,
  A wise and cautious hoard.

My youth is but a summer's day,
Then like the bee and ant, I'll lay
  A store of learning by;
And though from flower to flower I rove,
My stock of wisdom I'll improve,
  Nor be a butterfly.

LESSON CXLV.

Rey' nard.   ven' ture.

The Fox in the Well.

A fox having fallen into a well contrived, by sticking his claws into the sides, to keep his head above water. Soon after, a wolf passing by came and peeped over the edge of the well. The fox begged him very earnestly in some way to help him get out. The wolf, seeming to pity the fox, replied; "Ah! poor Reynard, I am sorry for you with all my heart. How came you to be so imprudent as to venture near this dangerous place?" "Nay, friend," said the fox, "if you feel as you say, do not stand pitying me, but lend me some aid as fast as you can. For pity is cold comfort when one is up to the chin in water, and within a hair's breadth of drowning."

Words are cheap. Not a few people are ready enough to *say* kind things to those who are in trouble, while they are very slow to

THE PRACTICAL

LESSON CXLVI.

Words ending in er, ar, and or, of two syllables, accented on the first.

Wā´ fer	hol ster	slen der	pil fer
wa ger	loi ter	ren der	gin ger
pa per	join er	ten der	pitch er
dra per	oys ter	ledg er	hith er
qua ver	vouch er	trench er	thith er
wa ver	full er	neth er	with er
ta per	can cer	teth er	bick er
game ster	slan der	weth er	flick er
dan ger	crack er	ves per	wick er
man ger	cank er	cen ser	prim er
cham ber	hank er	shel ter	sim per
lay er	ant ler	wel ter	fil ter
e ther	scam per	en ter	shiv er
fe ver	ham per	fes ter	liv er
east er	pam per	pes ter	sliv er
bea ver	tam per	tem per	riv er
bri er	ban ter	lep er	quiv er
ci der	can ter	ev er	splin ter
spi der	chap ter	lev er	win ter
vi per	sal ver	clev er	sis ter
mi ser	sam pler	nev er	pon der
so ber	gan der	sev er	yon der
o ver	pan ther	el der	host ler)
clo ver	chand ler	ped ler	ost ler)
dro ver	gath er	sil ver	nec tar
gro cer	lath er	lim ber	vic ar
bro ker	rath er	tim ber	mor tar
port er	mem ber	cin der	pop lar
col ter	fend er	hin der	vul gar
hol ster	gen der	tin der	cō dar

va por	fla vor	o dor	can dor
li ar	sa vor	hu mor	val or
po lar	ra zor	ru mor	clam or
so lar	may or	tu mor	hor ror
lu nar	tre mor	stu por	act or
la bor	pri or	ju ror	fac tor
ma jor	mi nor	tu tor	cap tor
fa vor	do nor	ran cor	lan guor *

* Pronounced lăng´ gwur.

LESSON CXLVII.

Words ending in er, ar, ir, yr, and or, of two syllables, accented on the first.

Lăd´ der	let ter	fod der	gram mar
blad der	fet ter	sod er	beg gar
ad der	sell er	of fer	cel lar
stam mer	tell er	cof fer	pil lar
ham mer	dif fer	prof fer	col lar
ban ner	glim mer	cop per	dol lar
man ner	sim mer	hop per	bur sar
tan ner	skim mer	tot ter	nā dir
bat ter	in ner	ot ter	sat yr
scat ter	din ner	pot ter	mar tyr
chat ter	spin ner	rob ber	zĕph yr
shat ter	sin ner	shud der	splen dor
tat ter	bit ter	rud der	ten or
flat ter	lit ter	blub ber	cen sor
mat ter	glit ter	drum mer	er ror
smat ter	frit ter	sum mer	ter ror
spat ter	tit ter	ut ter	debt or
wrap per	twit ter	but ter	rec tor
pep per	slip per	gut ter	fer vor
bet ter	dip per	flut ter	vic tor

LESSON CXLVIII.

Words ending in er and or, of two syllables, accented on the first.

Mŭt′ ter	lob ster	but ler	farm er
sput ter	song ster	cut ler	char ter
stut ter	con quer	huck ster	har bor
cut ter	fos ter	tum bler	par lor
shut ter	cum ber	bŭtch er	pas tor
sup per	lum ber	fȧ ther	ar bor
up per	slum ber	far ther	ar dor
suf fer	num ber	gar ner	ar mor
gun ner	ul cer	ȧf ter	rĭg or
crŭp per	un der	raft er	vig or
ŏr der	thun der	bar ter	liq uor
bor der	blun der	gar ter	mir ror
for mer	plun der	plas ter	hon or
cor ner	sun der	arch er	tor por
mon ster	mur der	bar ber	doc tor
both er	fur ther	part ner	spon sor
prop er	mus ter	mas ter	suc cor
pros per	clus ter	an swer	sculp tor

What word ends in *uor* ?

LESSON CXLIX.

Words ending in or and er, of three syllables, accented variously.

Mē′ te or	sen a tor	de mēan′ or
coun sel lor }	or a tor	di vi şor
coun sel or }	ed i tor	cre a tor
băch e lor	cred i tor	spec ta tor
chan cel lor	an ces tor	dic ta tor
gov ern or	mon i tor	tes ta tor
em per or	viş it or }	e qua tor
con quer or	viş it er }	trans la tor

sur vi vor }	wag on er	ob ject or
sur vi ver }	mes sen ger	con tract or
nar ra tor	scav en ger	pro ject or
prŏv′ en der	cū cum ber	in struct or }
cyl in der	jew el ler }	in struct er }
por rin ger	jew el er }	e lect or
can is ter	di a per	col lect or
bal us ter	uş u rer*	in spect or
in te ger	păss o ver	di rect or
sin is ter	har bin ger	cal′ en dar }
bar ri er	ar bi ter	kal en dar }
far ri er	grass hop per	vin e gar
bar ris ter	gar den er	sim i lar
mar i ner	con dŭct′ or	tab u lar
al mo ner	en am or	glob u lar
cor o ner	pre cur sor	sec u lar
mil li ner	suc cess or	oc u lar
min is ter	con fess or	cĭr cu lar
pass en ger	pro fess or	mŭs cu lar
＿res by ter	ag gress or	reg u lar
kid nap per	trans gress or	an gu lar†
trav el ler }	op press or	sin gu lar†
trav el er }	as sess or	pop u lar
sor cer er	pos sess or	in su lar

* Pronounced yū′ zhu rer.
† Pronounced ăng′ gu lar, sĭng′ gu lar.

LESSON CL.

Words ending in or and er, of three and four syllables, accented variously.

Pro tĕct′ or	Sep tem ber	ven ti lā′ tor
pre cept or	Oc tō ber	spec u la tor
in vent or }	No vĕm ber	cal cu la tor
in vent er }	De cem ber	reg u la tor

tor mĕnt´ or	re mĕm´ ber	mod e ra´ tor
im pos tor	in cum ber	nu me ra tor
a bet tor	con sid er	ar bi tra tor
in fē´ ri or	be wil der	im i ta tor
su pe ri or	sur ren der	nav i ga tor
an te ri or	dis or der	com men ta tor
ul te ri or	dis tem per	cul ti va tor
in te ri or	se ques ter	con ser va tor
ex te ri or	dis sev er	pros e cu tor
pos te ri or	de liv er	per se cu tor
pro pri e tor	ex cheq uer	co ad ju tor
am băs sa dor)	diş ås ter	pred e cĕs sor
em bas sa dor)	re māin der	in ter ces sor
pro gen i tor	em broid er	mal e fac tor
in quiş i tor	di ăm´ e ter	ben e fac tor
com poş i tor	ther mom e ter	ca lum ni ā´ tor
ex poş i tor	ba rom e ter	de nom i na tor
com pet i tor	ad min is ter	ad min is tra tor
con trib u tor	pa rish ion er	ver năc´ u lar
con spir a tor	i dol a ter	o rac u lar
su per vī´ şor	as tron o mer	par tic u lar
al li ga tor	a dul ter er	pen in su lar
in sti ga tor	ar tif i cer	cat´ er pil lar
gla di a tor '	up hōl ster er	per pen dic´ u lar

LESSON CLI.

Words ending in re and er.

Lū´ cre (kĕr)	fi bre	lus tre
a cre	måu gre	thē´ a tre
li vre	scĕp tre	sĕp ul chre
sa bre *	spec tre	mas sa cre
me tre	cen tre	re con noi´ tre
mi tre	som bre	am phi thē´ a tre

* Also spelt saber, meter, &c.

LESSON CLII.

I' dle.　　chil' dren.　　com pan' ion.　　bus' y.　　les' son.

Industry and Idleness.

Who'll come and play with me, here under the tree,
　My sisters have left me alone ;
My sweet little sparrow, come hither to me,
　And play with me, while they are gone.

O, no, little truant, I can't come, indeed,
　I've no time to idle away,
I've got all my dear little children to feed,
　And my nest to new cover with hay.

Pretty bee, do not buzz about over that flower,
　But come here and play with me, do ;
The sparrow wont come and stay with me an hour,
　But say, pretty bee—will not you ?

O, no, little truant, for do you not see
　Those must work who would prosper and thrive,
If I play they would call me a sad, idle bee,
　And perhaps turn me out of the hive.

Stop ! stop ! little ant, do not run off so fast,
  Wait with me a little and play ;
I hope I shall find a companion at last,
  You are not so busy as they.

O, no, little truant, I can't stay with you,
  We're not made to play, but to labor ;
I always have something or other to do,
  If not for myself, for my neighbor.

What then !' have they all some employment but me,
  Who lie lounging here like a dunce ?
O, then, like the ant, and the sparrow and bee,
  I'll go to my lesson at once.

LESSON CLIII.
Words ending in cy, sy, and zy.

Rā' cy	ce lib a cy	de gen e ra cy
flee cy	the oc ra cy	a ris toc' ra cy
i cy	de moc ra cy	ēa' sy
spi cy	con spir a cy	greas y
sâu cy	ef' fi ca cy	dai sy
mĕr cy	del i ca cy	nois y
pol' i cy	in tri ca cy	ro sy
proph e cy	prof li ga cy	drow sy
leg a cy	in ti ma cy	flĭm sy
fal la cy	con tu ma cy	quin sy
bank rupt cy	ob sti na cy	gip sy
pī ra cy	ac cu ra cy	tip sy
lu na cy	ob du ra cy	drop sy
se cre cy	id i o cy	tan sy
pri va cy	ef fem' i na cy	clum sy
di plo' ma cy	e pis co pa cy	phren sy }
su prĕm a cy	con fed e ra cy	fren zy . }

ec′ sta sy   court e sy   con tro ver sy
em bas sy   pleū ri sy   lā′ zy
lep ro sy   dys pĕp′ sy   ha zy
jeal ous y   hy poc′ ri sy   ma zy
proph e sȳ   a pos ta sy   cra zy
her e sy   ep′ i lep sy   dĭz zy

What words end in zy ?

LESSON CLIV.

Words ending in an, en, eign, ain, and on.

Hū′ man	strait en	si phon
pa gan	li ken	ci on
ŏr gan	swol len	rĭb bon ⎞
tur ban	o men	rib and ⎬
sul tan·	ri pen	rib in ⎠
pū′ ri tan	o pen	flag on
lu the ran	molt en	wag on
ăl co ran	has ten	beck on
vet e ran	chas ten	reck on·
pub li can	chief tain	tal on
ár ti şan	fount ain	mel on
par ti şan	mount ain	gal lon
guard i an	chăp lain	lem on·
a grā′ ri an	cap táin	salm on
co me di an	mur rain	gam mon
col le gi an	cer tain	mam mon
ra′ ven	cur tain	com mon
hea then	vil lain	sum mon
wi den	for eign	ser mon
deaf en *	băr gain	can non
hy phen	bā con	gram mā′ ri an
weak en	bea con	li bra ri an
maid en	dea con	sec ta ri an

* Some pronounce dĕf′ en.

his to ri an   brĕth ren   drăg on
tra ge di an   kit ten   mat ron *
re pŭb li can   glad den   pat ron *
mo ham me dan   sad den   per son
me rid i an   red den   ten don
e ques tri an   wax en   ten on
pe des tri an   kitch en   can on
the o lō´ gi an   tō ken   saf fron
pres by te ri an   co lon   cit ron
e pis co pa´ li an de mon   priṣ on
an te di lu vi an   a pron   dam ṣon
ha´ ven   rea ṣon   crim ṣon
e ven   trea ṣon   les son
clo ven   ma son   pis ton
wo ven   poi ṣon   cot ton
bra zen   cray on   bŭt ton
fro zen   bla zon   glut ton

* Others pronounce mā´ tron, pā´ tron.

What words end in ain? in sign? in and?

LESSON CLV.
Words ending in en, in, ine, and on.

Bĭd´ den   lin en   mit ten
hid den   hap pen   writ ten
trod den   as pen   rot ten
sod den   bar ren   sev en
sud den   les sen   gàr den
bur den   oft en   hard en
chil dren   ox en   heark en
chick en   list en   fàll en
strick en   glis ten   em bōld´ en
tick en   fat ten   a cu men
striv en   flat ten   en light en
sul len   smit ten   be to ken

en li ven   mat in   mu'ton
e lĕv en   mȧr gin   pȧr son
ab' do men   ŏr' i gin   par don
cit i zen   as sas' sin   jar gon
bā' sin   me theg lin   o rī' on
ru in   en' gine   en vi ron
raiş in   fam ine   ho ri zon †
rŏb in   er mine   a băn don
ur chin   rap ine   ū' ni son
vĭr gin   doc trine   chăm pi on
fir kin   des tine   scor pi on
căb in   san guine *   cin na mon
bob bin   vac cĭne   grid i ron ‡
bod kin   med' i cine   and i ron ‡
cof fin   dis ci pline   moc ca son
muf fin   mas cu line   gar ri son
nap kin   jes sa mine ⎫   skel e ton
gob lin   jas mine ⎬   pen ta gon
pip pin   fem i nine   oc ta gon
pump kin   her o ine   pol y gon
muş lin   nec ta rine   cri tē' ri on
reş in ⎫   līb er tine   al lu vi on
roş in ⎭   gen u ine   ob lĭv i on
sat in   de ter' mine   phe nom e non
spav in   pre des tine   com par i son
jave lin   in tes tine   sem i cō' lon
ver min   il lū mine   dăn' de lī on

* Pronounced săng' gwin.

† Some hŏr' i zon.   ‡ Pronounced grĭd' i urn, ănd' i urn.

In the following words geon and gion are pronounced jŭn,
and cheon, chŭn.

Dŭn' geon   sur geon   blud geon   cŭsh ion
lun cheon   stur geon   lē gion   făsh ion
pun cheon   dud geon   re gion   con tā' gion

LESSON CLVI.
Words ending in ure and eur.

Nā′ ture	pict ure	pást ure
creat ure	strict ure	joint ure
feat ure	tinct ure	pro cēd′ure
moist ure	script ure	dis fīg ure
fu ture	fixt ure	con text ure
fail ure	mixt ure	ad mixt ure
stăt ure	fig ure	con ject ure
fract ure	in jure	de bent ure
capt ure	tort ure	in dent úre
rapt ure	post ure	ad vent ure
lect ure	junct ure	im post ure
gest ure	punct ure	con junct ure
vest ure	struct ure	de párt ure
cinc ture	cult ure	man u făct′ ure
text ure	vult ure	no men clāt ure
verd ure	rupt ure	ăg′ ri cult ure
per jure	sculpt ure	hor ti cult ure
ten ure	nurt ure	per ad vent′ure
vent ure	grand eur	su per struct ure

What word ends in *eur?*

LESSON CLVII.
Words ending in ance and ence.

Frā′ grance	ac cept′ ance	dil′ i gence
guid ance	ob ṣerv ance	pest i lence
clear ance	re ṣist ance	em i nence
nui sance	as sist ance	prom i nence
griev ance	ad mit tance	con ti nence
sĕm blance	re mit tance	ab sti nence
pen ance	ac cord ance	pen i tence
venge ance	con cord ance	prev a lence

de fī′ ance	al lē′ gi ance	per ma nence
af fi ance	lux u rī ance	def er ence
re li ance	ex trăv a gance	ref er ence
al li ance	pre pond er ance	pref er ence
com pli ance	pre dom i nance	dif fer ence
ap pli ance	cā′ dence	in fer ence
en dur ance	cre dence	con fer ence
in sur ance *	pru dence	rev er ence
as sur ance *	sci ence	com pe tence
o bei sance	si lence	con se quence
con triv ance	vi′ o lence	ex pē′ ri ence
ac quaint ance	ve he mence	be nĕf i cence
an noy ance	åu di ence	in tel li gence
pur su ance	ĭn no cence	ir rev er ence
con niv ance	con fi dence	ma lev o lence
al low ance	res i dence	be nev o lence
re şĕm blance	ev i dence	im per ti nence
at tend ance	prov i dence	mag nif i cence
re mem brance	in di gence	mu nif i cence
re pent ance	neg li gence	co in ci dence

* Pronounced in shūr′ ans; as shūr′ ans.

LESSON CLVIII.
Words ending in ance and ence.

Băl′ ance	ut′ ter ance	af′ flu ence
rid dance	ig no rance	in flu ence
dis tance	com plais ance	con flu ence
in stance	rā di ance	con dō′ lence
pit tance	va ri ance	ad he rence
ord nance	main te nance	co he rence
sub stance	coun te nance	de pĕnd ence
per form′ ance	de lĭv′ er ance	in dul gence
re mŏn strance	con tĭn u ance	ef ful gence
im port ance	in her it ance	di verg ence

dis turb ance   ap pur' te nance   ab hor' rence
a bund ance   per se vē' rance   oc cur rence
re dund ance   ăb' sence   sub sist ence
re pug nance   es sence   con sist ence
in cum brance   preṣ ence   ex cres cence
re luct ance   sen tence   ac qui es' cence
cog' ni zance *   ex' cel lence   con va les cence
el e gance   in do lence   ef fer ves cence
ar ro gance   in so lence   rem i nis cence
pet u lance   im po tence   cor re spond ence
or di nance   el o quence   om ni preṣ ence
sus te nance   im pu dence   in ad vert ence
dis so nance   tur bu lence   ju ris prū dence
hin der ance   cor pu lence   in ter fe rence
fur ther ance   op u lence   con cu' pis cence
tem per ance   vir u lence   cir cŭm fe rence

* Some pronounce cŏn' i zance.

LESSON CLIX.

Words ending in ancy and ency.

Făn' cy   re gen cy   de pend en cy
vā' can cy   co gen cy   de spond en cy
pli an cy   flu en cy   con tin gen cy
poign an cy   fre quen cy   e merg en cy
in fan cy   tĕnd en cy   con sist en cy
con stan cy   pun gen cy   de lin quen cy
nec' ro man cy   urg en cy   ap' pe ten cy
oc cu pan cy   clem en cy   ex cel len cy
dis crep' an cy   cur ren cy   ex i gen cy
pre cip' i tan cy solv en cy   in no cen cy
sig nif i can cy   com plā' cen cy   preṣ i den cy
dē' cen cy   trans par en cy   ex pē' di en cy
a gen cy   as cĕnd en cy   sub sĕrv i en cy

LESSON CLX.
The Storm.

A violent gale is blowing through the woods. This oak, which had stood firm for more than a hundred years, as if proud of its strength, would not yield to the blast. Its stout trunk is broken in the middle, and it is falling to the ground.

That young elm seems to feel the force of the storm, and wisely bending its trunk and branches, remains unhurt.

One man, like the oak, defies the gale. He loses his hat and cloak, and is himself nearly blown over. He, too, may fall to the ground.

The other man sees that it will do no good to try to resist the blast. He yields to it, and goes back again. The storm will soon be over, and he will turn about and go on his way safely.

Better bend than break.

Proverbs.

He that makes light of *small* sins, is in danger of falling into *great* ones.

Better to be alone than in bad company.

Rely not on *another* for what you can do yourself.

He that is discontented cannot find an easy seat.

He that speaks ill of *others* to me, will also speak ill of *me* to others.

A *proud* man has no God; an *envious* man has no neighbor; an *angry* man has not himself.

Oil and truth will get uppermost at last.

Single drops make up the sea.

One may *talk* like a wise man, and yet *act* like a fool.

A bad workman quarrels with his tools.

Every light is not the sun.

He that is good at making excuses, is seldom good for any thing else.

Turn a deaf ear to a backbiter.

He that peeps through a hole, *may* see something to vex him.

A good name is better than riches.

If you seek to lie upon *roses* when young, you may have to lie upon *thorns* when you are old.

LESSON CLXI.

Words ending in ate, of three syllables, accented on the first.

Cĕl′ e brāte	pen e trate	sup pli cate
em a nate	per pe trate	fab ri cate
ex ca vate	dem on strate *	ex tri cate
ag gra vate	com pen sate *	mas ti cate
prop a gate	con tem plate *	im pli cate
dev as tate *	en er vate *	rus ti cate
dep re cate	al ter nate	can di date
im pre cate	ul cer ate	liq ui date
dep re date	tol er ate	ob li gate
con gre gate	gen er ate	ir ri gate
des e crate	ven er ate	lit i gate
ex e crate	ab di cate	mit i gate
lib e rate	med i cate	cas ti gate
op e rate	in di cate	in sti gate

* Others accent these on the second syllable.

nav i gate	grav i tate	cĭr cu late
ven ti late	sal i vate	mŏd u late
vac ci nate	cul ti vate	reg u late
fas ci nate	cap ti vate	em u late
nom i nate	med i tate	stim u late
crim i nate	des ig nate	rec re ate
germ i nate	ex tir pate *	pop u late
term i nate	im mo late	sat u rate
dis si pate	stip u late	am pu tate
em i grate	sup pu rate	un du late
im mi grate	sub ju gate	vī o late
mil i tate	con ju gate	po ten tate
im i tate	ed u cate	fu mi gate
ir ri tate	spec u late	mu ti late
heş i tate	cal cu late	ăr bi trate

* Some accent this on the second syllable.

LESSON CLXII.

Words ending in ate, of three and four syllables, accented variously.

Il lŭs' trāte	com mu ni cate	e rad i cate
in un date	e lu ci date	pre var i cate
in cul cate	il lu mi nate	au then ti cate
ex cul pate	ac cu mu late	do mes ti cate
pro mul gate	a măl ga mate	prog nos ti cate
re mon strate	re ver ber ate	in tox i cate
a pos tate	pre pon der ate	in val i date
con cen trate	vo cif er ate	con sol i date
un der rāte'	ac cel er ate	in tim i date
re in state	i tin er ate	di lap i date
va ri' e gate	co op er ate	in vest i gate
e nu me rate	com miş er ate	as sim i late
re mu ner ate	re it er ate	con tam i nate
an ni hi late	ob lit er ate	dis sem i nate

re crim i nate   de bil i tate   com mem o rate
dis crim i nate   fa cil i tate   e vap o rate
a bom i nate   de cap i tate   in cor po rate
pre dom i nate   ne ces si tate   ex pec to rate
de nom i nate   re cip ro cate   ges tic u late
ex term i nate   e quiv o cate   in oc u late
as sas si nate   ac com mo date   co ag u late
e man ci pate   in ter ro gate   de pop u late
pro cras ti nate   in ter po late   con grat u late
re sus ci tate   cor rob o rate   ca pit u late
pre med i tate   in vig o rate   ex pos tu late

LESSON CLXIII.

Words ending in ate, of two, three, and four syllables, accented variously.

Prī′ vate   del i cate   in test ate
pi rate   as pi rate   con sum mate
cli mate   ob sti nate   col lē′ gi ate
pro bate   in tri cate   im me di ate
cu rate   prox i mate   in vi o late
păl ate   prof li gate   con sĭd er ate
ag ate   ul ti mate   in vet er ate
man date   choc o late   il lit er ate
leg ate   cor po rate   ef fem i nate
sen ate   con su late   in or di nate
frig ate   for tu nate   le git i mate
dū′ pli cate   ac cu rate   dis con so late
o pi ate   ob du rate   e lect o rate
ăd e quate   in car nate   im mac u late
des pe rate   ap pel late   im port u nate
tem per ate   al ter nate   com men su rate

He that is slow to anger is better than the mighty; and he that ruleth his spirit, than he that taketh a city.

LESSON CLXIV.

When the following words are used as verbs, *a* in ate is long;
when used as nouns or adjectives, it is obscure.

Sĕp' a rate	in ti mate	re gen er ate
del e gate	an i mate	cer tif i cate
con se crate	con fis cate	pre cip i tate
ag gre gate	ad vo cate	pre des ti nate
mod er ate	des o late	de term i nate
ded i cate	rep ro bate	sub or di nate
pred i cate	con fed' er ate	ap prox i mate
com pli cate	de gen er ate	e lab o rate
es ti mate	de lib er ate	ar tic u late

LESSON CLXV.

In the following words, ci and ti before ate have the sound
of sh, and when they follow i this sound is united with the
preceding syllable in pronunciation; as vi'tiate, pronounced
vĭsh' ate.

Sā' tiate	as so ciate	ob vi ate
vĭ tiate	ne go tiate	ac tu ate
in i' tiate	ex cru ciate	fluc tu ate
pro pi tiate	li cen tiate	punc tu ate
no vi tiate	e nun ciate	grad u ate
of fi ciate	rā' di ate	sit u ate
in grā tiate	me di ate	de lin' e ate
in sa tiate	de vi ate	re tal i ate
ex pa tiate	spo li ate	con cil i ate
e ma ciate	ro se ate	ca lum ni ate
ap pre ciate	nau se ate *	ab brē vi ate
de pre ciate	rec re ate	al le vi ate
con so ciate	pal li ate	ir ra di ate

* Pronounced naw' she āt. Others, naw' shāt.

re pu di ate	lux u ri ate	in sin u ate
in e bri ate	ac cĕn tu ate	e vac u ate
ap pro pri ate	at ten u ate	in fat u ate
in fu ri ate	ex ten u ate	per pet u ate

What words end in *ciate*?

LESSON CLXVI.

Words ending in any, eny, iny, and ony.

Bŏt' a ny	eb o ny	ig no min y
lit 'a ny	sym pho ny	cer e mo ny
tyr an ny	fel o ny	ac ri mo ny
vil lain y	col o ny	mat ri mo ny
des ti ny	glut ton y	pat ri mo ny
mū ti ny	ī ro ny	test i mo ny
scru ti ny	lär ce ny	pär si mo ny
băl co ny	har mo ny	ma hŏg' a ny
ag o ny	mĭs' cel la ny	mo not o ny

LESSON CLXVII.

Words ending in ary, ery, ory, and ury, of three syllables,
accented on the first.

Dī' a ry	beg ga ry	found er y
li bra ry	con tra ry	gro cer y
pri ma ry	gloss a ry	droll er y
ro şa ry	bur gla ry	rail ler y *
ro ta ry	sum ma ry	ärch e ry
no ta ry	drā per y	ar te ry
vo ta ry	brav er y	chan ce ry
roşe ma ry	knav er y	băt ter y
ple nà ry	slav er y	flat ter y
bound a ry	scen er y	gal ler y
săl a ry	brib er y	quack er y
gran a ry	fi er y	rev er y ⎫
sect a ry	fin er y	rev er ie ⎭

* Some pronounce răl' ler e.

ev er y	drudg er y	his to ry
im age ry	sur ger y	sā vor y
fish er y	gun ner y	the o ry
slip per y	but ter y	i vo ry
frip per y	num ner y	ȧr mor y
mis er y	nurs er y	ū su ry*
liv er y	mys te ry	åu gu ry
sor ce ry	mem o ry	pĕn u ry
mock er y	pleth o ry	cen tu ry
crock er y	rec tor y	mer cu ry
or re ry	pil lo ry	per ju ry
lot ter y	cur so ry	in ju ry
rob ber y	fac to ry	lux u ry
shrub ber y	vic to ry	treas ur y*

* Pronounced yū′ zhu re, trĕzh′ ur e.

LESSON CLXVIII.

Words ending in **ary**, **ery**, and **ory**, of four syllables, accented variously.

Brēv′ i a ry	sem i na ry	form u la ry
mo ment a ry	san guin a ry	sub lu na ry
cu li na ry	vi sion a ry *	vol un ta ry
lu mi na ry	mis sion a ry *	trib u ta ry
ȧr bi tra ry	em is sa ry	sal u ta ry
mĕr çe na ry	com mis sa ry	Jan u a ry
lit er a ry	mil i ta ry	Feb ru a ry
ad ver sa ry	sol i ta ry	stat u a ry
plan et a ry	dig ni ta ry	sanc tu a ry
sec re ta ry	an ti qua ry	sump tu a ry
sed en ta ry	hon or a ry	sal u ta ry
com men ta ry	tem po ra ry	es tu a ry
sec ond a ry	pul mo na ry	mon as ter y
or di na ry	cus tom a ry	cem e ter y

* Pronounced vĭzh′ un a re, mĭsh′ un'a re.

dys en ter y	in ven to ry	ro ta to ry
mil li ner y	rep er to ry	de lu' so ry
pres by ter y	prom is so ry	il lu so ry
pred a to ry	dor mi to ry	re frăct o ry
pref a to ry	ter ri to ry	re fect o ry
pur ga to ry	trans i to ry	di rect o ry
or a to ry	prŏm on to ry	ac ces so ry
dil a to ry	des ul to ry	per emp to ry
hor ta to ry	nŭ ga to ry	con sist o ry
al le go ry	mi gra to ry	com pul so ry

LESSON CLXIX.

Words ending in ary, ery, and ory, of four, five, and six syllables, accented variously.

Ac cĕs' sa ry	man u fac to ry
dis pens a ry	sat is fac to ry
in fĭrm a ry	in ter ces so ry
cŏr'ol la ry	val e dic to ry
a pŏth' e ca ry	con tra dic to ry
sub sid i a ry	in tro duc to ry
in cen di a ry	ex' pi a to ry
pre lim i na ry	ded i ca to ry
he red i ta ry	lab o ra to ry
de pos i ta ry	sup pli ca to ry
im ag i na ry	de fam' a to ry
e pis to la ry	de clam a to ry
co tem po ra ry	in flam ma to ry
vo cab u la ry	ex plan a to ry
re sid u a ry	de clar a to ry
o bit u a ry	pre par a to ry
vo lup tu a ry	com mend a to ry
dis' ci pli na ry	ob serv a to ry
an ni vers' a ry	ob lig a to ry
par lia ment a ry	de rog a to ry

test a ment' a ry   con sol' a to ry
el e ment a ry   pro hib i to ry
com pli ment a ry   de poş i to ry
sup ple ment a ry   ad mon i to ry
rev o lū' tion a ry   pre mon i to ry
su per nu mer a ry   sa lu ta to ry
per fum' er y   in ter rŏg' a to ry
çhi can er y   re tal' i a to ry
de bȧuch er y   con cil i a to ry
a dŭl ter y   con grat u la to ry

LESSON CLXX.

The Self-made Man.

More than a hundred years ago, a man lived in Scot
land, whose name was Edmund Stone. His father wa
poor, and worked in the garden of a rich man. This mar
one day, found a learned book in Latin on the grass, an
inquired to whom it belonged. He was told that it wa
young Edmund's. He was much astonished to find tha
the son of the gardener could read Latin, and understan
such a book. He said to him, " How came you to kno
all these things ?"

" A servant," replied the young man, (who was the
eighteen years old,) " taught me to read ten years ag

Does one need to know any thing more than the twenty-six letters, to learn every thing else that he wishes ?"

The rich man was still more surprised, as he received from Edmund this further account.

"I first learned to read," said he, "when the masons were at work on your house. Standing by them, one day, I observed that the builder used a rule and compass, and that he made figures on a slate. I asked what was the use of his doing so, and was told that by learning arithmetic, which enabled him to do this, I could do the same. So I bought a book and learned arithmetic. I was told there was another science, called geometry; and getting the proper books, I learned that too. By reading, I found there were good books in Latin which taught arithmetic and geometry. So I bought a dictionary, and learned Latin. I understood, still further, that there were good books of the same kind in French. I bought a dictionary, and learned French. This, Sir, is what I have done. It seems to me, that we can learn every thing, when we know the twenty-six letters of the alphabet."

Edmund, afterwards, became a very learned man and a distinguished writer of books ;—showing what a resolute and persevering boy can accomplish. How many other boys might do the same.

LESSON CLXXI.

In the following words ending in ous, geous and gious have the sound of jŭs ; as gor' geous, pronounced gŏr' jŭs.

Fā' mous	mon strous	ri ot ous
fi brous	cum brous	co pi ous
pi ous	vā' ri ous	glo ri ous
po rous	de vi ous	o di ous
joy ous	pre vi ous	o dor ous
căl lous	se ri ous	cu ri ous
ner vous	te di ous	du bi ous
lep rous	li bel lous ⎱	du te ous
pom pous	li bel ous ⎰	fu ri ous

hu mor ous	mur der ous	con gru ous
lu di crous	pit e ous	cred u lous
lu mi nous	plen te ous	em u lous
mu ti nous	pros per ous	fab u lous
nu me rous	rav en ous	pop u lous
ru in ous	slan der ous	rapt ur ous
scru pu lous	en vi ous	scrof u lous
spu ri ous	im pi ous	stren u ous
dan ger ous	ob vi ous	sumpt u ous
trait or ous	om i nous	trem u lous
bois ter ous	per il ous	so nō′ rous
pois on ous	scur ril ous	post hu mous
boun te ous	spir it ous	dis as trous
moun tain ous	mis chiev ous	por tĕn tous
bar bar ous	dec o rous *	stu pen dous
mar vel lous ⎰	clam or ous	tre men dous
mar vel ous ⎱	friv o lous	e nor mous
ar du ous	ven om ous	gor′ geous
scăn dal ous	glut ton ous	con tā′ gious
chiv al rous	ran cor ous	cour a geous
haz ard ous	rig or ous	out ra geous
vil lain ous	tim or ous	e gre gious
gen er ous	val or ous	ad van ta′ geous
hid e ous	vig or ous	right′ eous †

* Others, de cō′ rous.   † Pronounced rī′ chus.

LESSON CLXXII.

In the following words, ci, ti, se, and sci, before ous, have the sound of sh; and when they follow ĕ or i, this sound is united with the preceding syllable in pronunciation, as prĕ′ cious, pronounced prĕsh′ us.

Spā′ cious	cau tious	frac tious
gra cious	nau seous	cap tious
spe cious	făc tious	anx ious *

* Pronounced ănk′ shus.

nox ious *　　　fe ro cious　　　fla gi tious
con scious　　　pre co cious　　　ju di cious
lus cious　　　con tĕn tious　　　ma li cious
ca pā' cious　　　li cen tious　　　nu tri tious
fal la cious　　　in fec tious　　　of fi cious
pug na cious　　　sen ten tious　　　per ni cious
au da cious　　　pre' cious　　　pro pi tious
lo qua cious　　　vi cious)　　　se di tious
ra pa cious　　　vi tious)　　　sus pi cious
sa ga cious　　　am bi' tious　　　av a ri' cious
te na cious　　　fac ti tious　　　ex pe di tious
vo ra cious　　　ca pri cious　　　su per sti tious
vex a tious　　　aus pi cious　　　con sci en tious
fa ce tious　　　de li cious　　　ef fi cā cious
a tro cious　　　fic ti tious　　　per ti na cious

* Pronounced nŏk' shus.
What word ends in *seous*?

LESSON CLXXIII.

Words ending in ous, of four, five, and six syllables, accented
variously.

Gre gā' ri ous　　　la bo ri ous
ne fa ri ous　　　me lo di ous
pre ca ri ous　　　no to ri ous
spon ta ne ous　　　op pro bri ous
im pe ri ous　　　vic to ri ous
in ge ni ous　　　cir cu i tous
mys te ri ous　　　for tu i tous
ob se qui ous　　　gra tu i tous
cen so ri ous　　　in ju ri ous
com mo di ous　　　pe nu ri ous
er ro ne ous　　　sa lu bri ous
fe lo ni ous　　　u su ri ous
har mo ni ous　　　vo lu mi nous

a năl o gous
ca lam i tous
mag nan i mous
mi rac u lous
u nan i mous
ad ven tu rous
com pend i ous
con tempt u ous
im pet u ous
in gen u ous
ne ces si tous
su per flu ous
tem pest u· ous
am phib i ous
as sid u ous
car niv o rous
con tin u ous
con spic u ous
con tig u ous
in iq ui tous
in sid i ous
in vid i ous
las civ i ous
per fid i ous
per spic u ous
pre cip i tous
pro mis cu ous

ri dic u lous
vo cif er ous
a nom a lous
a non y mous
i dol a trous
pre pos ter ous
ca lum ni ous
il lus tri ous
in dus tri ous
pre sump tu ous
tu mult u ous
vo lup tu ous
spir' it u ous
sub ter rā' ne ous
si mul ta ne ous
in stan ta ne ous
mis cel la ne ous
ho mo ge ne ous
cer e mo ni ous
ac ri mo ni ous
mer i to ri ous
par si mo ni ous
pu sil lăn i mous
ig no min i ous
o do rif er ous
ex tem po rā' ne ous
het e ro ge ne ous

LESSON CLXXIV.

Words ending in ity, ety, and uty, of three, four, and five syllables, accented variously.

Lā' i ty	pău ci ty	grav i ty
de i ty	ăm i ty	suav i ty
u ni ty	cav i ty	van i ty

sanc ti ty	a cer bi ty	tran quil li ty
ver i ty	as per i ty	u biq ui ty
brev i ty	ad ver si ty	u til i ty
len i ty	ce leb ri ty	neu tral i ty
lev i ty	ce ler i ty	sta bil i ty
en mi ty	dex ter i ty	in iq ui ty
eq ui ty	fi del i ty	vi cin i ty
dig ni ty	fra ter ni ty	ma lig ni ty
com i ty	in teg ri ty	com mod i ty
jol li ty	lon gev i ty	e nor mi ty
prob i ty	ne ces si ty	fri vol i ty
pol i ty	pos ter i ty	pom pos i ty
par i ty	pro pen si ty	pro fun di ty
an nū' i ty	pros per i ty	gāy' e ty)
cre du li ty	te mer i ty	gai e ty)
con gru i ty	a bil i ty	pi e ty
com mu ni ty	a gil i ty	ni ce ty
gar ru li ty	ac cliv i ty	moi e ty
im mu ni ty	a vid i ty	sŭb til ty *
im pu ni ty	be nig ni ty	rick et y
sa lu bri ty	cu pid i ty	dep u ty
gra tu i ty	de cliv i ty	va ri' e ty
va cu i ty	fa cil i ty	sa ti e ty
bar băr i ty	fu til i ty	e bri e ty
a lac ri ty	gen til i ty	so bri e ty
ca lam i ty	hu mil i ty	anx i e ty †
hi lar i ty	no bil i ty	so ci e ty
ur ban i ty	fer til i ty	pro pri e ty
ex trem i ty	ster il i ty	con tra ri' e ty
prox im i ty	se ren i ty	no to ri e ty

When the last syllable but two ends in *i* or *y*, the termination is *ety*, as is also the case in *rickety* and *subtlety*; when otherwise, it is *ity*.

* Others, sŭb' tle ty, pronounced sŭt' tl ty.

† Pronounced ang zī' e ty.

What words end in *ity*? in *ety*? in *uty*?

LESSON CLXXV.

Words ending in ity, of five and six syllables, accented variously.

As si dū' i ty

am bi gu i ty

con ti gu i ty

in ge nu i ty

su per flu i ty

spon ta ne i ty

hos pi tăl i ty

af fa bil i ty

ca pa bil i ty

cul pa bil i ty

du ra bil i ty

e qua nim i ty

feas i bil i ty

flex i bil i ty

im be cil i ty

li a bil i ty

mag na nim i ty

mu ta bil i ty

pla ca bil i ty

plau si bil i ty

pos si bil i ty

prob a bil i ty

sens i bil i ty

u na nim i ty

u ni vers i ty

vers a til i ty

vol a til i ty

vol u bil i ty

cred i bil i ty

con san guin i ty

cu ri os i ty

gen er os i ty

me di oc ri ty

an i mos i ty

im mu ta bil' i ty

im pla ca bil i ty

ir ri ta bil i ty

prac ti ca bil i ty

res pect a bil i ty

com pat i bil i ty

di vis i bil i ty

el i gi bil i ty

LESSON CLXXVI.

In the following words, c at the end of a syllable preceding i, has the sound of s ; as ca pac' i ty, pronounced ca păs' i ty.

Ca păc' i ty

lo quac i ty

o pac i ty

ra pac i ty

sa gac i ty

te nac i ty

ve rac i ty

vi vac i ty

pug nac i ty

fe lic i ty

sim plic i ty	in flam ma bil' i ty
du plic i ty	in flex i bil i ty
rus tic i ty	in vin ci bil i ty
ve loc i ty	per fec ti bil i ty
a troc i ty	pu sil la nim i ty
fe roc i ty	re spon si bil i ty
per ti nac' i ty	sus cep ti bil i ty
ec cen tric i ty	im pen e tra bil' i ty
e lec tric i ty	in cor ri gi bil i ty
e las tic i ty	in tel li gi bil i ty
au then tic i ty	in cor rupt i bil i ty
mul ti plic i ty	in vi o la bil i ty
rec i proc i ty	in com pre hen si bil' i ty

LESSON CLXXVII.

In the following words, sion has the sound of zhŭn, and tion, of shŭn.

Suā' sion	le ga tion
per sua' sion	do na tion
dis sua sion	po ta tion
oc ca sion	no ta tion
ab ra sion	o ra tion
e va sion	mu ta tion
in va sion	du ra tion
per va sion	gra da tion
mis per sua' sion	ci ta tion
na' tion	pri va tion
ra tion	sal va tion
sta tion	de fal ca' tion
pro ba' tion	av o ca tion
car na tion	rev o ca tion
vo ca tion	per tur ba tion
ces sa tion	com pli ca tion
pur ga tion	in vo ca tion

con vo ca tion
prov o ca tion
con se cra tion
trep i da tion
ob li ga tion
spo li a tion
con ge la tion
rev e la tion
ap pel la tion
con stel la tion
dis til la tion
trib u la tion
pec u la tion
ad u la tion
stran gu la tion
def a ma tion
dec la ma tion
proc la ma tion
in flam ma tion
prof a na tion
ex pla na tion
in dig na tion
res ig na tion
ap pro ba tion
com bi na tion
or di na tion
in cli na tion
dec li na tion
div i na tion
cor o na tion
in to na tion
con ster na tion
con dem na tion
des ti na tion

rep a ra tion
prep a ra tion
con fla gra tion
im i ta tion
min is tra tion
an no ta tion
men su ra tion
hab i ta tion
vis i ta tion
al le ga tion
os ten ta tion
dis ser ta tion
ex hor ta tion
ex cla ma tion
ref u ta tion
rep u ta tion
der i va tion
dep ri va tion
val u a tion
co rus ca tion
e men da tion
res er va tion
pres er va tion
dis pen sa tion
re nun ci a' tion
de nun ci a tion
e jac u la tion
dis sim u la tion
con cat e na tion
hal lu ci na tion
per e gri na tion
in ter pre ta tion
pre med i ta tion
re sus ci ta tion

con tin·u a tion	in ter lin e a′ tion
ma nip u la tion	su per er o ga tion
al lit e ra tion	rec on cil i a tion

How many words, and what are they, that end in *asion*? Can you find
any others with the same termination? If not, all other words ending in
ion, (the accented syllable of which ends in *a*,) end in *tion*

LESSON CLXXVIII.

Examples of words ending in ation, derived from verbs ending
in y; tion having the sound of shŭn.

Oc cu pā′ tion	ver si fi ca tion
va ri a tion	pu ri fi ca tion
ap pli ca tion	rat i fi ca tion
mul ti pli ca′ tion	grat i fi ca tion
clas si fi ca tion	sanc ti fi ca tion
ed i fi ca ti on	for ti fi ca tion
mod i fi ca tion	mor ti fi ca tion
am pli fi ca tion	jus ti fi ca tion
sig ni fi ca tion	in dem ni fi ca′ tion
nul li fi ca tion	per son i fi ca tion

LESSON CLXXIX.

In the following words, sion has the sound of zhŭn,—tion and
cian, of shŭn; and when preceded by *i*, *zh* and *sh* are united
in pronunciation with the preceding syllable.

Ad hē′ sion	vĭ′ sion	col li sion
in he sion	re vi′ sion	cir cum ci′ sion
co he sion	di vi sion	am bi′ tion
de ple tion	pro vi sion	tra di tion
re ple tion	de ci sion	ad di tion
com ple tion	pre ci sion	e di tion
se cre tion	in ci sion	se di tion
ac cre tion	ex ci sion	con di tion
dis cre tion *	e li sion	per di tion

* Pronounced dis krĕsh′ un.

vo li tion	dem o li tion	rep e ti tion
ig ni tion	rec og ni tion	com pe ti tion
mo ni tion	def i ni tion	su per sti tion
con tri tion	ad mo ni tion	in tu i tion
at tri tion	pre mo ni tion	de com po şi' tion
nu tri tion	am mu ni tion	in ter po şi tion
mu ni tion	dis qui şi tion	ma gi' cian
tran si tion *	ac qui şi tion	lo gi cian
par ti tion	in qui şi tion	mu şi cian
fru i tion	ap po şi tion	phy şi cian
tu i tion	dep o şi tion	pa tri cian
pe ti tion	prep o şi tion	op ti cian
sus pi cion	im po şi tion	pol i ti' cian
pro hi bi' tion	com po şi tion	rhet o ri cian
ex hi bi tion	prop o şi tion	mech a ni cian
ex pe di tion	op po şi tion	a rith me ti' cian
er u di tion	sup po şi tion	a cad e mi cian
co a li tion	trans po şi tion	ge om e tri cian
eb ul li tion	dis po şi tion	math e ma ti' cian
ab o li tion	ex po şi tion	met a phy şi cian

* Pronounced tran sǐzh' un.

What words end in *cion?* and in *cian?* Those which end in *cian* denote agents. Can you find any others ending with a similar sound that also denote agents?

LESSON CLXXX.

In the following words, sion has the sound of zhŭn, and tion of shŭn.

Ex plō' sion	e mo' tion	af fu' sion
cor ro sion	com mo tion	ef fu sion
mo' tion	de vo tion	dif fu sion
no tion	lo co mo' tion	in fu sion
lo tion	o' cean *	con fu sion
po tion	fu sion	trans fu sion

* Pronounced ō' shun.

con clu sion	so lu tion	ev o lu tion
ex clu sion	ret ri bu´ tion	rev o lu tion
de lu sion	con tri bu tion	in vo lu tion
al lu sion	dis tri bu tion	dim i nu tion
il lu sion	pros e cu tion	sub sti tu tion
col lu sion	per se cu tion	des ti tu tion
pro fu sion	ex e cu tion	res ti tu tion
in tru sion	el o cu tion	in sti tu tion
con tu sion	ab so lu tion	con sti tu tion
ab lu tion	res o lu tion	cau´ tion
pol lu tion	dis so lu tion	pre cau´ tion

What word ends in *cean?*

LESSON CLXXXI.

In the following words si, ti, and ci, have the sound of sh; ssi
has also the same sound, united in pronunciation with the
accented syllable.

Măn´ sion	con ten tion	in cur sion
pen sion	dis ten tion	ex cur sion
ex pan´ sion	at ten tion	an i mad ver´ sion
as cen sion	pre ven tion	pōr´ tion
de clen sion	in ven tion	ap por´ tion
di men sion	ver´ sion	pro por tion
sus pen sion	sub mer´ sion	de şer tion
dis sen sion	im mer sion	in ser tion
pre ten sion	as per sion	as ser tion
ex ten sion	dis per sion	con tor tion
con de scen´ sion	a ver sion	dis tor tion
rep re hen sion	sub ver sion	ex tor tion
com pre hen sion	re ver sion	co er cion
ap pre hen sion	di ver sion	pas´ sion
men´ tion	in ver sion	ses sion
de ten´ tion	con ver sion	mis sion
in ten tion	per ver sion	ces sion

com pas' sion	trans gres sion	com mis sion
ac ces sion	de pres sion	o mis sion
suc ces sion	im pres sion	per mis sion
se ces sion	com pres sion	dis mis sion
con ces sion.	op pres sion	trans mis sion
pro ces sion	sup pres sion	con cus sion
con fes sion	ex pres sion	per cus sion
pro fes sion	pos ses sion	dis cus sion
ag gres sion	sub mis sion	in ter ces' sion
di gres sion	ad mis sion	pre pos ses sion
in gres sion	e mis sion	in ter mis sion
pro gres sion	re mis sion	man u mis sion

What words end in *tion?* in *cion?* Can you find any other words besides *suspicion* and *coercion* that end in *cion?*

LESSON CLXXXII.

In the following words sion,—and tion when not preceded by s,—have the sound of shŭn; xi, of ksh; and tion preceded by s, of chŭn.

Com pŭl' sion	de scrip tion	su per scrip' tion
re pul sion	tran scrip tion	ac' tion
ex pul sion	in scrip tion	fac tion
re vul sion	re demp tion	frac tion
con vul sion	pre emp tion	sanc tion
cap' tion	re sump tion	sec tion
op tion	pre sump tion	dic tion
de cep' tion	con sump tion	fic tion
re cep tion	as sump tion	fric tion
con cep tion	a dop tion	func tion
per cep tion	ab sorp tion	suc tion
ex cep tion	e rup tion	unc tion
as crip tion	ir rup tion	auc tion
pro scrip tion	cor rup tion	de jĕc' tion
sub scrip tion	dis rup tion	pro tec tion

con nec tion }	der e lic tion	in tro duc tion
con nex ion }	ben e fac tion	flex' ion
re duc tion	stu pe fac tion	flux ion
se duc tion	rar e fac tion	com plex' ion
sub trac tion	pu tre fac tion	cru ci fix' ion
de struc tion	pet ri fac tion	ques' tion
com punc tion	res ur rec tion	sug ges' tion
ju ris dic' tion	pre di lec tion	di ges tion
ben e dic tion	in sur rec tion	com bus tion

Are there any words that end in *ktion?* any that end in *psion?* any that end in *csion?*

LESSON CLXXXIII.

The Happy Family.

Oh! sweet as vernal dews that fill
The closing buds on Zion's hill,
   When evening clouds draw thither—
So sweet, so heavenly 'tis to see
The members of one family
    Live peacefully together.

The children, like the lily flowers,
On which descend the sun and showers.

Their hues of beauty blending;
The parents, like the willow boughs,
On which the lovely foliage grows,
Their friendly shade extending.

But leaves the greenest will decay,
And flowers the brightest fade away,
When autumn winds are sweeping;
And be the household e'er so fair,
The hand of death will soon be there,
And turn the scene to weeping.

Yet leaves again will clothe the trees,
And lilies wave beneath the breeze,
When spring comes smiling hither;
And friends who parted at the tomb,
May yet renew their loveliest bloom,
And meet in heaven together.

LESSON CLXXXIV.

In the following words i before a vowel has the sound of y;
as sēn' ior, pronounced sēn' yur.

Sēn' ior	pann ier	span iel
jun ior	val iant	ax iom
cloth ier	brill iant	pon iard
fol io *	bill iards	in dian
al ien	christ ian	ruff ian
sav ior	fust ian	mill ion
un ion	bil ious	pill ion
court ier	fil ial	trill ion
bull ion	best ial	bill ion
cŏll ier	cord ial	min ion

* Or. fō' li o.

pin ion	punc til io	o pin ion
on ion *	se ragl io	punc til ious
pe cūl' iar	ci vil ian	re bell ious
be hav ior	pa vil ion	brill' ian cy
con ven ient	pōst ill ion	mēl ior ate
com mun ion	ver mil ion	al ien ate
ple be ian	bat tall ion	pe cun' ia ry
ce lĕst' ial	re bell ion	aux īl ia ry
fa mil iar	com pan ion	fa mil iar ize
e lyş ium *	do min ion	christ ian i ty

* Pronounced ŭn' yun, e lĭzh' yum.

LESSON CLXXXV.

In the following words si, zi, and s have the sound of zh.

Glā' zier	ăz ure	treas ur y
gra zier	meas ure	vis u al
bra sier	pleas ure	ū su al
o sier	treas ure	dis clo' sure
ho sier	treas' ur er	e ra sure

LESSON CLXXXVI.

In the following words, s before u,—sci, si, ci, and ti, have the sound of sh.

Pā' tient	cen sure	ne go tia ble
an cient	sens' u al	pro por tion ate
pa tience	sō cia ble	af fĕc tion ate
ra tio	sta' tion a ry	con fec tion er
quo tient	dīc tion a ry	so cia bil' i ty
trăn sient	cen sur a ble	pen i ten tia ry
sen tient	stā tion e ry	pro bā' tion a ry
con science	in sa' tia ble	ob jĕc tion a ble

What word ends in cient? What words end in ary? What one in ery?

LESSON CLXXXVII.

In the following words, ci, sci, ti,—and ss before u and i,—have the sound of sh, which is united in pronunciation with the accented syllable.

Prĕss' ure	om nis cience	ju di cia ry
fis sure	mi li tia	prac ti tion er
de fi' cient	pas' sion ate	su per fi' cieṣ
ef fi cient	de fi' cien cy	ben e fi' cia ry
suf fi cient	ef fi cien cy	dis cre' tion a ry
pro fi cient	suf fi cien cy	in i tia to ry
om nis cient	pro fi cien cy	pro pi tia to ry

LESSON CLXXXVIII.

In the following words, used only in the plural, the final s, when not preceded by c or t, has the sound of z.

Tăc' tics	eaves	sham bles
eth ics	drĕgs	cal ends
phyṣ ics	tongs	vī tals
op tics	an' nals	twee zers
hys ter' ics	en trails	mea ṣles
i tal ics	em bers	wa ges
sta tis tics	nip pers	trowṣ ers
math e mat' ics	pin cers	bow els
rick' ets	snuff ers	spĕc' ta cles
ef fects'	scis ṣors	prem i ses
clōthes	ash es	mo lăs' ses }
stays	gog gles	me las ses }
shears	rich es	en vī rons

LESSON CLXXXIX.

The following words are pronounced as if h preceded w.

Whĭp	whist	which	whirl
whim	whisk	whipt	whĕn
whit	whiff	whĭr	whelp

whence	wheeze	whăt	whif fle
whet	whine	whărf	whis tle
whiz	white	whĕth′ er	whit tle
whāle	why	whisk er	whith er
whey (āy)	while	whim per	whēē dle
wheat	whilst	whis per	whĭm′ și cal
wheel	where	whit low	o ver whelm′

LESSON CXC.

To the following words, ending in ic, the termination al is not added.

Pŭb′ lic	cŏl ic	gym nas tic
dor ic	fab ric	spaș mod ic
gas tric	an tic	ter rif ic
ep ic	tū nic	con cen tric
civ ic	lu′ na tic	vŏl can ic
goth ic	plĕth o ric	re pub lic
frol ick }	bish op ric	e met ic
frol ic }	cath o lic	a quat ic
ton ic	e clip′ tic	ath let ic
pan ic	i tal ic	rheu mat ic
plas tic	phleg mat ic	pro șā ic
rel ic	ec lec tic	ca thăr tic
traf fick }	gi gan tic	dip lo măt′ ic
traf fic }	do mes tic	me te or ic
ărc tic	pa cif ic	pat ri ot ic
gar lic	prog nos tic	tel e graph ic

LESSON CXCI.

The following words are not varied so as to end in ic.

Lō′ cal	fis cal	met ri cal
fo cal	rad′ i cal	ver ti cal
vo cal	prac ti cal	drop si cal
răs cal	med i cal	sur gi cal

fin i cal
in im' i cal
non sen si cal
sym met ri cal

re cip ro cal
e quiv o cal
pi rat i cal
le vit i cal.

or a tor' i cal
di a met ri cal
prob lem at i cal
par a dox i cal

LESSON CXCII.

The following words are sometimes, though seldom, used with
the addition of al.

Cū' bic
mĭm ic
hec tic
rus tic
mim ick (verb.)
la con' ic
ge ner ic
ex trin sic
in trin sic
ec cen tric
pe dan tic

or gan ic
mo nas tic
er rat ic
ec stat ic
di dac tic
spe cif ic
nar cot ic
syl lab ic
*p*neu mat ic
me tal lic
pris̱ mat ic

pro lif ic
mag net ic
e las tic
ep i dem' ic
tel e scop ic
lith o graph ic
ar o mat ic
pan e gyr ic
id i ot ic
par a lyt ic
cli mac' ter ic

LESSON CXCIII.

The following words are sometimes, though seldom, used
without the termination al.

Clĕr' i cal
eth i cal
tec*h* ni cal
typ i cal
spher i cal
nău ti cal
ty răn' ni cal
i ron i cal
the at ri cal
sta tis ti cal

de ist i cal -
me thod i cal
gram mat i cal
i den ti cal
so phist i cal
ca non i cal
e van gel' i cal
ge o graph i cal
hy per bol i cal
ec o nom i cal

met a phor i cal
ge o met ri cal
met a phys i cal
math e mat i cal
hy po thet i cal
hy po crit i cal
jes̱ u it i cal
ex e get i cal
as tro nom i cal
al le gor i cal

LESSON CXCIV.

The following words are also used with the addition of al.

Mū' sic	sa tir ic	ac a dem ic
sto ic	his tor ic	a pos tol ic
ru bric	e lec tric	pu ri tan ic
grăph ic	em phat ic	at mos pher ic
com ic	dra mat ic	al pha bet ic
trop ic	sab bat ic	em ble mat ic
top ic	dog mat ic	sys te mat ic
lyṝ ic	sar cas tic . ..	e nig mat ic
clas sic	ma jes tic	mis an throp ic
phyṣ ic	nu mer ic	sym pa thet ic
mys tic	fan tas tic ⎫	ty po graph ic
crit ic	phan tas tic ⎬	syl lo gis tic
op tic	fa nat ic	dem o crat ic
cyn ic	· po et ic	en er get ic
scep tic ⎫	des pot ic	the o crat ic
skep tic ⎬	el lip tic	an a lyt ic
scen ic	pa thet ic	pan to mim ic
rhet' o ric	pro phet ic	par a bol ic
pol i tic	em pir ic	phil an throp ic
her e tic	he rō ic	a rith' me tic
an gel' ic	mo ṣa ic	hi e ro glyph' ic
sym bol ic	pe ri ŏd' ic	a ris to crat ic
pŏ lem ic	sci en tif ic	id i o mat ic
bo tan ic	phil o soph ic	en thu ṣi as tic
hys ter ic	di a bol ic	ec cle ṣi as tic

LESSON CXCV.

Words ending in cle, kle, and kel.

Cîr' cle	pin na cle	spec ta cle	i ci cle ⎫
ŭn cle	mir a cle	ob sta cle	i si cle ⎬
man' a cle	or a cle	ve hi cle	tu ber cle

bår na cle	shac kle	sic kle	an kle
ar ti cle	tac kle	tic kle	ran kle
par ti cle	spec kle	stic kle	crin kle
re cĕp' ta cle	frec kle	buc kle	sprin kle
con ven ti cle	fic kle	chuc kle	wrin kle
tab' er na cle	pic kle	knuc kle	tin kle
twin' kle	pric kle	truc kle	spår kle
cac kle	tric kle	suc kle	shĕk el

Do any words of more than two syllables end in *kle*? What word ends in *kel*?

LESSON CXCVI.

Words ending in cel, cle, cil, sel, sil, sal, cile and sile.

Căn' cel	ves sel	pro po şal
chan cel	tēaş el	dis po şal
mus cle *	weaş el	pe ru şal
pen cil	coun sel	re fu şal
pår cel	coun cil	es pou şal
cŏd' i cil	fŏs sil	ca rou şal
dom i cil	u ten' sil	re vĕrs al
chiş' el	vas' sal	u ni vers' al
dam şel	mis sal	dŏ' cile †
tin sel	nā şal	mĭs sile
mor sel	re pri' şal	pen sile
tas sel	sur pri şal	im' be cile †

* Pronounced mŭs' sl. † Others, dŏs' il, im bĕs' sil.

What words end in *cle*? in *cel*? and in *sile*?

LESSON CXCVII.

Words ending in bal, bel, bol, and ble.

Cўm' bal	lā bel	bab ble	grum ble
verb al	li bel	bub ble	hob ble
herb al	sўm' bol	am ble	hum ble
can' ni bal	gam bol	crum ble	jum ble
reb' el	bram ble	gam ble	nib ble

nim ble	stub ble	fee ble	går ble
peb ble	stum ble	ga ble	mar ble
quib ble	thim ble	bi ble	as sĕm′ ble
rab ble	trem ble	foi ble	dis sem ble
ram ble	tum ble	no ble	re şem ble
rum ble	ā ble	sa ble	en ā ble
scram ble	ca ble	sta ble	ig no ble
scrib ble	fa ble	ta ble	pre′ am ble

What words end in *al, el,* and *ol ?*

LESSON CXCVIII.

Words ending in able, uble, and ible, variously accented.

Prŏb′ a ble	pŏs si ble
pass a ble	sens i ble
af fa ble	viş i ble
syl la ble	cred i ble
ten a ble	tan gi ble
cul pa ble	fal li ble
pal pa ble	hor ri ble
ar a ble	ter ri ble
par a ble	flex i ble
not a ble	fōr ci ble
tract a ble	cru ci ble
tax a ble	fea şi ble
sol u ble	plău şi ble
vol u ble	ĕl′ i gi ble
fōrd a ble	ad miss′ i ble
sal a ble	com press i ble
blam a ble	de fens i blĕ
ca pa ble	di viş i ble
e qua ble	os ten si ble
du ra ble	re spons i ble
cu ra ble -	in del i ble

mū′ ta ble	com bus′ ti ble
port a ble	com pat i ble
suit a ble	cor rupt i ble
li a ble	con tempt i ble
teach a ble	con vert i ble
prăc′ ti ca ble	de struc ti ble
pred i ca ble	di gest i ble
am i ca ble	per cep ti ble
ap pli ca ble	i ras ci ble
des pi ca ble	in vin ci ble
ex pli ca ble	dis cern i ble
rev o ca ble	de dū ci ble
for mi da ble	in cŏr′ ri gi ble
nav i ga ble	in tel li gi ble
es ti ma ble	in ex press′ i ble
ad mi ra ble	ir re press i ble
ex e cra ble	ir re vers i ble
hon or a ble	rep re hen si ble
mem o ra ble	con tro vert i ble
miş er a ble	ir re sist i ble
in de fat′ i ga ble	in com pre hen′ si ble

What words end in *able?* If there are cognate words ending in *ant, ance, ate,* or *ation,* the adjective ends in *able.* If there are cognate words ending in *ist, ive, ision,* or *ition,* the adjective ends in *ible.* The exceptions are definable, supposable, resistible, and irresistible.

LESSON CXCIX.

Words ending in able, of four syllables, variously accented.

Prĕf′ er a ble	ex pi a ble
ref er a ble	pit i a ble
tol er a ble	val u a ble
ven er a ble	cred it a ble
vul ner a ble	eq ui ta ble
mal le a ble	hab i ta ble
en vi a ble	hos pi ta ble

im i ta ble   as sail a ble
lam en ta ble   de sir a ble
pal a ta ble   ac count a ble
prof it a ble   in dict a ble
pleas ur a ble*   in scru ta ble
par don a ble   con ceiv a ble
an swer a ble   de ceiv a ble
fa vor a ble   per ceiv a ble
a mi a ble   re triev a ble
va ri a ble   al low a ble
rea son a ble   re doubt a ble
sea son a ble   com mend a ble
trea son a ble   in flam ma ble
im pla' ca ble   con form a ble
sup po sa ble   im preg na ble
ex cu sa ble   de mon stra ble
a void a ble   ob serv a ble
a me na ble   trans fer a ble
re claim a ble   ac cept a ble
as sign a ble   de test a ble
at tain a ble   in ef fa ble
ob tain a ble   in tract a ble
a do ra ble   re spect a ble
de plo ra ble   re mark a ble

* Pronounced plĕzh' ur a bl.

LESSON CC.

Words ending in able, of five syllables, variously accented.

In ĕx' tri ca ble   con sid er a ble
in cal cu la ble   in com pa·ra ble
a bom i na ble   in ex o ra ble
de term i na ble   in sep a ra ble
in term i na ble   in suf fer a ble
ex cep tion a ble   ir rep a ra ble

im pen e tra ble	re me di a ble
un ut ter a ble	in dis pĕns' a ble
in dom i ta ble	mon o syl la ble
in ev i ta ble	in con test a ble
dis tin guish a ble	jus ti fī a ble
ex tin guish a ble	ir re proach a ble
in vī o la ble	un con troll a ble
in su per a ble	rec on cil a ble
in nu mer a ble	in sup port a ble
in du bi ta ble	in sur mount a ble

Adjectives in able, derived from words ending in e, are spelt without the e before a; except when, as in the following examples, the primitive ends in ce, ge, or ee.

Pēace' a ble	sĕr' vice a ble
trace a ble	man age a ble
change a ble	mar riage a ble
chárge a ble	a grēē' a ble

LESSON CCI.

Words of two syllables, ending in al, el, ail, il, ile, ule, ul, ol, and le, accented on the first.

Mĕd' al	mod el	cav il	ea gle
san dal	grav el	civ il	sta ple
scan dal	rav el	an vil	ma ple
form al	trav el	tran quil	sŭp ple
nor mal	lev el	ten dril	scrū ple
dis mal	shriv el	per il	bu gle
sig nal	swiv el	nos tril	bee tle
ver nal	hov el	ē vil	ti tle
mor al	nov el	pu pil	păd dle
cen tral	grov el	A pril	strad dle
as tral	cam el	pro file	sad dle
met al	tram mel	fe brile	med dle

den tal	flăn nel	fū tile	pĕd dle
men tal	chan nel	sĕr vile	fid dle
mor tal	pau el	fer tile	mid dle
fes tal	ken nel	duc tile	rid dle
ves tal	fen nel	rep tile	hud dle
crys tal	fun nel	ster ile	pud dle
brī dal	tun nel	fer ule	can dle
feu dal	chap el	con sul	dan dle
na val	gos pel	car ol	han dle
ri val	min strel	pis tol	kin dle
o val	tim brel	ī dol	spin dle
re gal	bar rel	vi ol	dwin dle
fru gal	squir rel*	la dle	swin dle
le gal	sor rel	cra dle	fon dle
pe nal	cud gel	i dle	bun dle
ve nal	sach el	bri dle	trun dle
fi nal	hatch el	nee dle	cur dle
spi nal	man tel	ri fle	hur dle
pa pal	chat tel	tri fle	baf fle
e qual	trav ail	sti fle	scuf fle

What words end in *ail?* in *ule?* *ul?* and *ol?*
* Pronounced skwĕr' rel.

LESSON CCII.

Words ending in al, el, le, il, and ile, of two and three syllables, accented variously.

Cŏr' al	vi tal	tri al	fu el
ō ral	to tal	loy al	cru el
spi ral	port al	roy al	gru el
neu tral	bru tal	ān gel	jew el
plu ral	re al	se quel	măr shal
ru ral	di al	scoun drel	mar vel
fa tal	vi al }	ha zel	char nel
na tal	phi al {	du el	shŭf fle

muf fle	am ple	this tle	sub tle † ⎫
ruf fle	sam ple	bris tle	sub til ⎬
an gle *	tram ple	gris tle	sub tile ⎭
dan gle	tem ple	jos tle	friz zle
man gle	dim ple	bus tle	daz zle
wran gle	pim ple	hus tle	driz zle
span gle	sim ple	bat tle	muz zle
stran gle	ap ple	cat tle	puz zle
tan gle	dap ple	rat tle	gar ble
sin gle	grap ple	tat tle	star tle
jin gle	rip ple	ket tle	mŭl' ti ple
shin gle	crip ple	met tle	prin ci ple
min gle	tip ple	net tle	dis cī' ple
tin gle	stop ple	set tle	e pĭs tle
bun gle*	pur ple	lit tle	a pos tle
gur gle	man tle	spit tle	em bez zle
strag gle	gen tle	brit tle	au tum nal
wrig gle	tur tle	tit tle	in fer nal
jog gle	myr tle	bot tle	ma ter nal
jug gle	cas tle	rus tle	pa ter nal
smug gle	nes tle	scut tle	fra ter nal
strug gle	pes tle	shut tle	e ter nal
trip le	wres tle	ax le	in ter nal

* The words from *angle* to *bungle*, inclusive, are pronounced as if the first syllable ended with *g*.

† Pronounced sŭt' tl.

LESSON CCIII.

Words ending in al, el, ile, and ol, of three syllables, accented variously.

Ar rī' val	ca the dral	de ni al
re vi val	re ci tal	tri bu nal
co e val	re qui tal	re new al
pri me val	i de al	a vow al

bap tiş mal   per son al   ar se nal
pa rent al   nom i nal   car di nal
ac quit tal   in te gral   pas tor al
di ur nal   ad mi ral   nū mer al
noc tur nal   tem po ral   fu ner al
ca tárrh al   cor po ral   la bi al
fēs' ti val   nat u ral   ge ni al
in ter val   script u ral me ni al
prod i gal   gut tu ral   jo vi al
con ju gal   cap i tal   cit a del
an i mal   hos pi tal   in fi del
or di nal   ped es tal   cal o mel
crim i nal   lin e al   sen ti nel
doc tri nal   or de al   di shev' el
prin ci pal   triv i al   en am el
lib er al   grad u al   em pan nel)
fed er al   an nu al   im pan nel)
gen er al   ac tu al   ap par el
min er al   rit u al   vol' a tile
lat er al   punc tu al   vers a tile
lit er al   vir tu al   pū er ile
sev er al   sex u al   căp i tol

What words end in *ile?* and *ol?*

LESSON CCIV.

Words ending in al, of four, five, and six syllables, accented variously.

Ac ci děnt' al   sup ple ment al
in ci dent al   sen ti ment al
o ri ent al   det ri ment al
fun da ment al   mon u ment al
sac ra ment al   in stru ment al
or na ment al   con ti nent al
el e ment al   hor i zon tal

di ag′ o nal
e phem er al
e lect or al
con ject ur al
ad verb i al
pro verb i al
bi en ni al
tri en ni al
mil len ni al
per en ni al
ter res tri al
con viv i al
re şid u al
con tin u al
ef fect u al
per pet u al
ha bit u al
e vent u al
in åug u ral
e thē re al
cor po real
fu ne re al
re me di al

con ge nial
a e ri al
ma te ri al
im pe ri al
me mo ri al
ar te ri al
mer cu ri al
su i ci′ dal
spĭr′ it u al
in di vid′ u al
in tel lect u al
in ter mē′ di al
min is te ri al
cer e mo ni al
mat ri mo ni al
pat ri mo ni al
test i mo ni al
sen a to ri al
e qua to ri al
mon i to ri al
ter ri to ri al
ex per i mĕnt′ al
me di a tō′ ri al

LESSON CCV.

In the following words ci, si, and ti have the sound of sh; and when ci and ti follow e or i, this sound is united with the preceding syllable in pronunciation.

Sō′ cial
pro vĭn′ cial
fi nan cial
com mer cial
pär′ tial
mar tial

nŭp tial
sub stan′ tial
cre den tial
pru den tial
es sen tial
e qui noc′ tial

cir cum stan tial
preş i den tial
prov i den tial
pes ti len tial
in flu en tial
con se quen tial

nā′ tion al   de vō tion al   su per fi cial
ra tion al   spĕ′ cial   in i′ tial
no tion al   ju di′ cial   sol sti tial
frăc tion al   of fi cial   tra di′ tion al
sec tion al   prej u di′ cial   ad di tion al
op tion al   ben e fi cial   con di tion al
in ten′ tion al   ar ti fi cial   con tro ver′ sial

LESSON CCVI.

In the following words ch has the sound of k.

Schēme   ech oeş   ȧrch e type
ache   pas chal   arch i tect
chyle   ȧr chīveş   harp si chord
school*   cha ŏt′ ic   hī e rarch
chăşm   scho las tic   pa tri arch
chord   me chan ic   eu cha rist
chā′ os   se pul chral   cha me′ le on
cho ral   arch ān gel   pa ro chi al
cho rus   chi me ra   cha lȳb e ate
e poch   chăr′ ac ter   chi mer i cal
te trarch   chol er ic   chi rog ra phy
schoon er*   chor is ter   chro nol o gy
chŏl er   chron i cle   chro nom e ter
christ en   chrys a lis   char ac ter ize
christ mas   al che my   mo nȧrch i cal
chron ic   an ar chy   ar′ chi tect ure
chem ist ⎫   cat e chįşe   ŏl i gar chy
chim ist ⎭   căt e chişm   mel an chol y
an chor   pen ta teuch   mel an chol ic
mon arch   chĕm is try ⎫   pa tri ȧrch′ al
sched ule   chim is try ⎭   mach i nā tion
schol ar   mech a nişm   cat e chu men
ech o   sac cha rine   char ac ter ĭs′ tic

* o, as in move.

LESSON CCVII.

In the following words ph has the sound of f.

Trī′ umph met a phor
tro phy eū′ pho ny
ty phus åu to graph
ci pher tri ŭm′ phant
dŏl phin tri um phal
eph od phi lip pic
soph ism de cī pher
ser aph bi ŏg′ ra phy
proph et bi og ra pher
or phan ste nog ra phy
cam phor or thog ra phy
pam phlet ge og ra phy
aph′ o rism ty pog ra phy
blas phe my phi los o phy
blas phe mous phi los o pher
ep i taph a poc ry phal
lith o graph phe nom e non
par a graph phi lan thro py
tel e graph e piph a ny
syc o phant lex i cog′ ra phy
soph is try phys i og no my

LESSON CCVIII.

In the following words, g at the end of syllables, and followed by e or i, has the sound of j; and c, in similar cases, that of s.

Lŏg′ ic dig it leg er ⎫
mag ic vig il ledg er ⎭
trag ic ag ile proc ess
rig id frag ile plac id
frig id tac it ac id

prog′ e ny	spec i fy	in dig e nous
veg e tate	im ag′ ine	veg′ e ta ble
ag i tate	e lic it	mag is tra cy
cog i tate	il lic it	leg is lat ure
vig il ance	so lic it	reg i ment al
leg i ble	im plic it	im ag′ in a ble
mag is trate	ex plic it	im ag in a tive
leg is late	an tic′ i pate	spec i fi ca′ tion
reg i men	par tic i pate	mag is te′ ri al
reg i cide	ca pac i tate	du o dĕc i mo
trag e dy	so lic i tude	an a log i cal
reg is ter	au dac i ty	ge o log i cal
fōrg er y	me dic in al	zo o log i cal
văç il late	mu nic i pal	phren o log i cal
tac i turn	rhi noc e ros	tau to log i cal
dec i mal	so lic it ous	the o log i cal
lac er ate	so lic it or	phi lo log i cal
prec i pice	nec′ es sa ry	chron o log i cal
prec e dent	rec i tā′ tion	et y mo log′ i cal
spec i men	o rĭg′ in ate	gen e a log i cal
rec i pe	bel lig▸er ent	min er a log i cal
pac i fy	o rĭg in al	phyş i o log i cal

LESSON CCIX.

In the following words x has the sound of gz; as ĕx′ hort, pronounced ĕgz′ hort.

Ex hŏrt′	ex ile	ex am ple
ex ist	ex hăust	ex am ine
ex empt	ex ălt	ex ot ic
ex êrt	ex hĭb′ it	ex or′ di um
ex act	ex em plar	ex hil a rate
ex ult	ex ist ence	ex on er ate
ex hāle	ex er tion	ex em pla ry

ex em pli fy   ex ec u tive   ex ū ber ance
ex orb i tance   ex ec u tor   ex as per ate
ex ag ger ate   ex ec u trix   ex am i nā′ tion

LESSON CCX.

Irregular and very difficult words, of which the particular pronunciation is given.

	Pronounced.		Pronounced.
Choir	kwīre	bus i ness	bĭz′ ness
folks	fōkes	bus i ly	bĭz′ ze ly
isle	īle	corps	kōre
is land	ī′ land	i ron	ī′ urn
aisle	īle	buoy	bwoy
schism	sĭzm	buoy ant	bwoy′ ant
bu ry	bĕr′ ry	pro vost	pro vō′
bu ri al	bĕr′ e al	ap ro pos	ăp′ ro pō
drachm	drăm	belle	bĕl
en glish	ĭng′ glish	spe cies	spē′ shiz
fore head	fŏr′ ed	co quet	ko kĕt′
man y	mĕn′ ny	co quette	*or* co quĕt′
an y	ĕn′ ny	vig net	vin yĕt′
phthis ic	tĭz′ zik	vig nette	
of	ŏv	yacht	yŏt
pret ty	prĭt′ ty	sold ier	sōl′ jur
plaid	plăd	sug ar	shŭg′ ar
been	bĭn	seign ior	sēen′ yur
rheum	rūme	worst ed	wŭst′ ed
rhyme	rīm	col o nel	kŭr′ nel
thyme	thīm or tīm	vict uals	vĭt′ tlz
rhythm	rĭthm	beau	bō
fran chise	frăn′ chiz	beaux	bōze
mi nu tiæ	me nū′ shē	does	dŭz
wom an	wŭm′ an	ven i son	vĕn′ zn
wom en	wĭm′ en	pig eon	pĭd′ jun
bus y	bĭz′ zy	mosque	mosk

	Pronounced.
kins folk	kĭnz′ fōke
haut boy	hō′ boy
schis mat ic	siz măt′ ic
mus ke toe mus que toe }	mus kē′ to
rhyth mi cal	rĭth′ mi cal
buoy an cy	bwoy′ an sy
et i quet et i quette }	et e kĕt′
bru nette	bru nĕt′
ga zette	ga zet′
hick up hic cough }	hĭk′ kup
pus tule .	{ pŭs′ l or pŭs′ tul
belles lettres	bĕl′ let ter
men ag er y	men āzh′ er ē
ex haus tion	egz haws′ chun
mis tle toe	mĭz′ zl tō
sou ve nír	soo′ ve nĕr *
av oir du pois	av er du poiz′
re lig ious	re lĭd′ jus
re lig ion	re lĭd′ jun
li tig ious	le tĭd′ jus
pro dig ious	pro dĭd′ jus
sac ri le gious	sak re lē′ jus
con ta gious	kon tā′ jus
bur lesque †	bur lĕsk′
gro tesque	gro tĕsk′
pic tu resque	pikt u rĕsk′
aid de camp	ād′ de kawng
gone	gŏn ; or nearly, gawn.

WORDS

Spelt alike, but which vary in Accent.

Signification when accented on the first syllable.		Signification when accented on the second syllable.
Not here.	*Absent.*	To keep away.
an abridgment.	*Abstract.*	to draw from.
a stress of voice.	*Accent.*	to express accent.
something added to the end of a word.	*Affix.*	to unite to the end.
an increase.	*Augment.*	to make larger.
the eighth month.	*August.*	grand.
a short prayer.	*Collect.*	to gather together.
an agreement.	*Compact.*	solid.
a mixture.	*Compound.*	to mix together.
a musical performance.	*Concert.*	to plan by mutual agreement.
behavior.	*Conduct.*	to lead.
limit.	*Confine.*	to restrain.
a struggle.	*Conflict.*	to strive against
to practise charms.	*Conjure.*	to implore.
a companion.	*Consort.*	to associate with.
a contention.	*Contest.*	to dispute.
a bargain.	*Contract.*	to lessen.
opposition of figures.	*Contrast.*	to set in opposition.
familiar discourse.	*Converse.*	to talk with.
one who adopts a new opinion.	*Convert.*	to change from one state to another.
a person proved guilty.	*Convict.*	to prove guilty.
an accompanying protection, usually by sea.	*Convoy.*	to accompany for protection, usually by sea.
a growing less.	*Decrease.*	to grow less.
a summary of laws.	*Digest.*	to arrange in order.
passage for entering.	*Entrance.*	to put in ecstasy.
a guard.	*Escort.*	to attend as a guard.
an attempt.	*Essay.*	to endeavor.
banishment.	*Exile.*	to banish.
a commodity sent to another country.	*Export.*	to carry goods to another country.
something drawn out.	*Extract.*	to draw out.
a commotion.	*Ferment.*	to excite internal motion.

Signification when accented on the first syllable.		Signification when accented on the second syllable.
happening often.	*Frequent.*	to visit often.
high spirited.	*Gallant.*	courteous to ladies.
meaning.	*Import.*	{ to bring from another country.
a mark.	*Impress.*	to stamp.
a perfume burnt.	*Incense.*	to make angry.
a growing larger.	*Increase.*	to grow larger.
a gross abuse.	*Insult.*	to treat abusively.
something noticed.	*Object.*	to oppose.
complete.	*Perfect.*	to make complete.
sweet odor.	*Perfume.*	to fill with sweet odor.
a written licence.	*Permit.*	to allow.
a particle put before a word.	*Prefix.*	to put before.
a solemn declaration.	*Protest.*	to affirm with solemnity.
one under government.	*Subject.*	{ to bring under the power of.
an attentive view.	*Survey.*	to view carefully.
anguish.	*Torment.*	to put to extreme pain.
a conveyance.	*Transfer.*	to convey.
a vessel for carriage; rapture.	*Transport.*	to carry; to enrapture.

WORDS

Spelt alike, but which vary in accent and division into syllables.

Cem' ent, that which unites.
Ce ment', to unite closely.
Des' ert, a wilderness.
De sert', to forsake.
Min' ute, a short space of time.
Mi nute', very small.
Pres' age, a prognostic.
Pre sage', to forebode.
Pres' ent, a gift.
Pre sent', to offer.
Prod' uce, that which is brought forth.
Pro duce', to bring forth.
Prog' ress, onward motion.
Pro gress' to advance.

Proj' ect, a scheme.
Pro ject', to be prominent.
Reb' el, one who renounces lawful authority.
Re bel', to renounce lawful authority.
Rec' ord, a register.
Re cord', to register.
Ref' use, of no value.
Re fuse', to deny a request.
At' tri bute, quality.
At trib' ute, to ascribe.
In val' id, of no force.
In' val id, } an infirm person.
In val id', }

WORDS

AIL, to be sick, or in trouble.
ale, a kind of malt liquor.
air, that which we breathe.
air, a tune; the manner of a person.
ere, before in time.
heir, one who inherits.
aisle, a walk or alley in a church.
isle, an island.
all, the whole.
awl, a sharp pointed tool.
altar, a place for sacrifice.
alter, to change.
ant, a small insect.
aunt, the sister of one's parent.
ark, a small chest; a vessel.
arc, a part of a circle.
ascent, a going up.
assent, agreement.
auger, a tool to bore with.
augur, one who foretells.
aught, any thing.
ought, bound in duty.
bad, not good, vicious.
bade, commanded.
bail, a surety.
bale, a bundle of goods.
bale, to lade out.
ball, a round body.
bawl, to cry aloud.
bare, without covering.
bear, a wild animal.
bear, to carry; to produce.
base, mean, vile.
base, the bottom or foundation.
bass, a part in music.
bay, a color; a body of water.
bey, a Turkish governor.
be, to exist.
bee, an insect which makes honey.
beach, the sea-shore.
beech, a kind of tree.
beat, to strike.
beet, an eatable root.
beau, a gay gentleman.
bow, an instrument to shoot with

been, from *be*; as, he has been.
bin, a box for commodities.
beer, a kind of liquor.
bier, a carriage for the dead.
bell, a hollow sounding body.
belle, an admired lady.
berry, a small fruit.
bury, to put under ground.
blew, from *blow*; as, the wind blew.
blue, a kind of color.
boar, a male swine.
bore, to make a hole, as with an auger.
boll, the pod of a plant, as of flax.
bowl, a round hollow vessel.
borne, from *bear*, to carry.
bourn, a limit.
borough, an incorporated town.
burrow, a hole for small animals.
bough, a branch.
bow, to bend.
brake, fern.
break, to force asunder.
breach, a breaking.
breech, the lower part of a thing.
bread, a kind of food.
bred, brought up.
broach, to pierce a vessel.
brooch, an ornament.
bruit, a noise, a report.
brute, a beast.
but, as, he has but one eye.
butt, a mark; to strike with the head.
butt, a cask containing two hogsheads.
buy, to get for money.
by, with, near.
bye, as, in good-bye.
Cain, the first murderer.
cane, a staff, or reed.
call, to name; to speak aloud.
caul, a membrane inclosing the bowels.
cannon, a great gun.
canon, a law, a rule.

canvas, a kind of cloth.
canvass, to examine.
　cask, a barrel to contain fluids.
　casque, a helmet.
cede, to give up.
seed, what produces plants.
　ceil, to cover the top or roof of a
　　room.
　seal, to fasten with a wafer, or wax.
　seal, an animal.
cell, a small apartment.
sell, to exchange for money.
　cent, a hundred ; a coin.
　scent, a smell.
　sent, ordered, or put in the way
　　to go.
cession, a giving up.
session, a sitting for business.
　choir, a band of singers.
　quire, 24 sheets of paper.
choler, anger, rage.
collar, a covering for the neck.
　chord, a line in a circle.
　cord, a small rope.
chronical, continuing long.
chronicle, a history.
　cion, a sprout.
　Sion, a mountain.
cite, to summon, to quote.
sight, vision, a view.
site, a situation.
　climb, to ascend with effort.
　clime, a portion of the earth.
coarse, not fine, rough.
course, the line of motion.
　coat, a part of dress.
　cote, a sheep-fold.
complement, a full number.
compliment, an expression of civ-
　　ility.
　core, the heart, or inner part of a
　　thing.
　corps, a body of men.
cousin, a relation.
cozen, to cheat.
　currant, a small fruit.
　current, a running stream.
cymbal, an instrument of music.
symbol, a sign.
　day, a portion of time.
　dey, a Moorish governor.

dear, beloved ; costly.
deer, a wild animal.
　dew, a kind of moisture.
　due, owed.
die, to cease to live in the body.
dye, to stain, to color.
　doe, a female deer.
　dough, meal prepared for baking.
done, finished.
dun, a dark color.
dun, to demand a debt.
　dram, a small weight.
　drachm, an ancient coin.
dam, to stop a stream.
damn, to condemn.
　ewe, a female sheep.
　yew, a kind of tree.
　you, the person, or persons, spo-
　　ken to.
eye, the organ of sight.
I, myself.
　fain, willingly.
　fane, a temple.
　feign, to dissemble.
faint, feeble, exhausted.
feint, a false appearance.
　fair, a place of sale ; beautiful,
　　just.
　fare, food ; price of passage.
feat, a striking action.
feet, the lower parts of the legs.
　flea, a troublesome insect.
　flee, to run away.
flew, from *fly* ; as, the bird flew.
flue, a passage for smoke.
　flour, meal from grain.
　flower, a blossom.
fore, going first.
four, twice two.
　forth, forward, out.
　fourth, next after the third.
foul, dirty, filthy.
fowl, a winged animal.
　freeze, to harden into ice.
　frieze, a coarse kind of cloth.
fir, a sort of tree.
fur, the soft hair of animals.
　gait, manner of walking.
　gate, a sort of door.
gilt, adorned with gold.
guilt, wickedness, crime.

grate, a frame made with bars.
great, large.
groan, a sound uttered in pain.
grown, increased.
  hail, frozen rain; to call, to salute.
  hale, to drag; sound in body.
hair, natural cover of the head.
hare, a small animal.
  hall, a large room.
  haul, to pull forcibly.
hart, a male deer.
heart, the seat of life.
  heal, to cure.
  heel, the hind part of the foot.
hear, to perceive by the ear.
here, in this place.
  heard, from *hear*; as, I heard it.
  herd, a drove or flock.
hew, to cut down.
hue, color; a clamor.
  hie, to move in haste.
  high, tall, lofty.
him, from *he*; as, I saw him.
hymn, a song of religious praise.
  hoard, to lay up in store.
  horde, a band of wandering peo-
    ple.
hole, a hollow place.
whole, having all its parts.
  hour, a portion of the day.
  our, belonging to us.
in, within.
inn, a tavern.
  indict, to charge with crime.
  indite, to write, to compose.
key, an instrument to fasten and
    open a lock.
quay, a wharf.
  kill, to take away life.
  kiln, a large stove or oven.
knave, a rogue.
nave, the middle of a wheel.
  knead, to work dough.
  need, want, necessity.
knew, from *know*; as, I knew him.
new, fresh, not old.
  knight, a title of honor.
  night, the darkness between the
    setting and the rising of the
    sun.
knit, to make network with needles.
nit, an insect's egg.

knot, a tie; a hard part in wood.
not, a word of denial or refusal.
know, to understand clearly.
no, a word of denial or refusal.
  laid, placed.
  lade, to load; to dip out.
lain, from *lie*, to rest, to remain.
lane, a narrow road or street.
  lea, a meadow.
  lee, opposite to the wind.
lead, a soft heavy metal.
led, guided, directed.
  leaf, a part of a plant.
  lief, willingly.
leak, to run out as a liquid.
leek, a sort of onion.
  lean, wanting flesh.
  lien, a claim on property.
lessen, to make less.
lesson, something to be read or
    learned.
  levee, an assembly to visit some
    distinguished person.
  levy, to raise money or troops;
    to collect.
liar, one who tells lies.
lyre, a musical instrument.
  lie, a wilful falsehood.
  lie, to recline, to rest.
  lye, a liquor from wood-ashes.
lo, behold.
low, near the ground; humble.
low, to make a noise like a cow.
  loan, to lend.
  lone, by itself, solitary.
lore, learning.
lower, to let down.
  made, finished.
  maid, an unmarried woman.
mail, armor; a bag to carry letters.
male, a he animal or plant.
  main, chief, principal.
  main, the ocean; the continent.
  mane, hair on the neck of animals.
maize, Indian corn.
maze, an intricate winding.
  mall, a wooden hammer.
  maul, to beat, to bruise.
manner, mode, custom.
manor, a lordship.
  mantel, a chimney-piece.
  mantle, a loose garment.

marshal, to arrange.
martial, warlike.
  mead, a liquor made from honey.
  meed, reward.
mean, a medium.
mean, low; to signify.
mien, look, air, manner.
  meat, animal food.
  meet, fit, proper.
  meet, to come together.
  mete, to measure.
metal, iron, silver, gold, &c.
mettle, spirit, ardor.
  might, power, ability.
  mite, a small insect.
moan, to lament aloud.
mown, from to mow; as, the grass
  is mown.
  moat, a ditch.
  mote, a small particle.
naught, bad.
nought, nothing.
  nay, no.
  neigh, to make a noise like a
    horse.
O, Oh, alas.
owe, to be indebted.
  oar, an instrument to row with.
  ore, metal as dug from the earth.
one, a single thing.
won, from win, to gain.
  pail, a wooden vessel.
  pale, a pointed stake; whitish,
    wan.
pain, suffering of body, or of mind.
pane, a square of glass.
  pair, a couple.
  pare, to cut off the outside.
  pear, a kind of fruit.
palate, a part of the mouth.
pallet, a small bed.
  panel, a part of a door
  pannel, a small saddle.
peace, quietness, calmness.
piece, a separated part.
  peak, the pointed top of a hill or
    mountain.
  peek, to look through a crevice.
  pique, a grudge.
peal, a loud sound.
peel, to skin, or take off the rind.

peer, an equal; a nobleman.
pier, a support of a bridge.
  plain, level ground; distinct, even.
  plane, a level surface; a tool.
plait, to fold, to double.
plate, wrought silver.
  plum, a fruit.
  plumb, a leaden weight.
pole, a long stick.
poll, the head; an election.
  pore, a small hole in the skin.
  pour, to turn out a liquid.
pray, to implore, to beseech.
prey, plunder, booty.
  principal, chief.
  principle, a fixed general truth.
profit, pecuniary or other advantage.
prophet, one who foretells.
  rain, water from the clouds.
  reign, to rule.
  rein, part of a bridle.
raise, to lift up, to elevate.
raze, to overthrow, to efface.
  rap, to strike.
  wrap, to fold together.
read, to peruse,
reed, a hollow knotted stalk.
  read, did read.
  red, a color.
reek, to smoke, to steam.
wreak, to take revenge.
  rest, repose; remainder.
  wrest, to force from.
retch, to strain.
wretch, a miserable person.
  rice, a kind of grain.
  rise, ascent, increase.
right, straight, just.
rite, a ceremony.
write, to form letters with a pen.
wright, a workman.
  ring, something circular.
  ring, to ring; as, he rings a bell.
  wring, to twist.
road, a way.
rode, from to ride; as, he rode on
  a horse.
  roe, a female deer.
  row, a rank; to move a boat with
    oars.

rote, a mere repetition of words.
wrote, from *write*; as, he wrote a letter.
rough, uneven, harsh.
ruff, a part of dress for the neck.
rout, a rabble.
route, } a way. (Some pronounce
rout, } this roote.)
rye, a kind of grain.
wry, crooked.
sail, a part of a ship.
sale, a selling.
scene, a sight.
seen, beheld.
sein, } a large fishing-net.
seine, }
scull, to propel a boat with an oar over the stern.
skull, the bone that incloses the brain.
sea, a large body of water.
see, to look at, to behold.
seam, two edges joined together.
seem, to appear.
sear, to burn to dryness.
sere, dry, withered.
seer, a prophet.
seignior, a lord.
senior, elder.
sew, to unite with a needle and thread.
so, in such a manner.
sow, to scatter seed.
shear, to clip, or cut off with a two-bladed instrument.
sheer, unmixed, pure.
shire, a county. (Some pronounce shīre.)
shone, from *shine*; as, the sun shone.
shown, from *show*; as, it was shown to me.
slay, to kill.
sleigh, a vehicle drawn on snow.
sley, a weaver's reed.
sleight, an artful trick.
slight, to neglect.
sloe, a sort of wild plum.
slow, not quick.
soar, to mount upward.
sore, painfully tender.

sole, single, only; the bottom of a foot or shoe.
soul, the immortal part of man
some, a part.
sum, the whole.
son, a male child.
sun, the great source of light.
stair, a step.
stare, to look earnestly.
stake, a post; a wager.
steak, a slice of meat.
stationary, fixed in place.
stationery, paper, ink, quills, &c.
steal, to take secretly and wrongfully.
steel, refined hardened iron.
stile, steps into a field.
style, manner of writing; to name.
straight, direct, not crooked.
strait, a narrow pass.
succor, help, aid.
sucker, a young shoot.
tail, the end.
tale, a story; a reckoning.
tare, an allowance in weight.
tear, to rend.
team, a number of horses or oxen for drawing.
teem, to abound, to produce.
tear, water shed from the eye.
tier, a rank, or row.
their, belonging to them.
there, in that place.
threw, from *throw*; as, he threw a stone.
through, as, he passed through the door.
throe, extreme pain.
throw, to cast.
throne, a royal seat.
thrown, from *throw*; as, the stone was thrown.
to, towards a place.
two, one and one.
too, also.
toe, a part of the foot.
tow, to drag with a rope, as a boat.
tow, the coarse part of flax or hemp.
travail, to labor.
travel, to go a journey.

vail, }
veil, } a covering for the face.
vale, a space between hills.
  vain, empty, showy, useless.
  vane, a weathercock.
  vein, a tube to convey the blood.
vial, }
phial, } a small bottle.
viol, a musical instrument.
  .vice, wickedness.
  vise, a griping instrument closed
    by a screw.
wail, to weep aloud.
wale, a mark of a stripe.
  wain, a wagon.
  wane, to decrease.

waist, the middle part of the body.
waste, desolate, to squander.
  wait; to tarry, to expect.
  weight, heaviness.
waive, to put off.
wave, a moving swell of water.
  ware, something to be sold.
  wear, to carry on the body, as
    clothes.
way, a manner; a road.
weigh, to find out how heavy a body
  is.
  weak, feeble, infirm.
  week, seven days.
wean, to withdraw from the breast.
ween, to think.

OF PREFIXES AND SUFFIXES.

A prefix is a letter, syllable, or word, placed at the beginning of a word, to vary its meaning; as *un* before able in *un*able, and *re* in *re*build.

A suffix is a letter, or syllable, annexed to the end of a word to modify its signification; as *ar* in begg*ar*, and *less* in father*less*.

In certain words, the prefixes and suffixes seem nearly or quite redundant.

OF THE PREFIXES.

Some of the prefixes drop or change their final consonant, so as to unite easily with the first syllable of the word to which they are joined; as *con* in *co*-exist, and *ad* in *af*-fix.

A denotes, *on, in, to, at,* or *from*; as, *a*shore, *a*bed, *a*field, *a*far, *a*vert.

Want of, or *without*; as, *a*theist.

Ab, abs —*from* or *away*; as, *ab*duce, *ab*stract.

Ad —*to* or *at*; as, *ad*join, *ap*pertain.

d in ad, becomes c, f, g, l, n, p, r, s, and t, in words beginning with these letters; as, *ac*cept, *al*lot.

Ante —*before*; as, *ante*date.

Anti —*against*; as, *anti*christian.

Circum —*about*; as, *circum*navigate.

Con, or its equivalents, co, cog, col, com, and cor —*together* or *with*; as, *con*form, *co*equal, *col*lect.

Contra, or counter —*against*; as, *contra*dict, *counter*part, *counter*mand.

De —*down* or *from*; as, *de*scend, *de*duct.

Dis, di, or dif —*take from, away, not*, or *asunder*; as, *dis*arm, *dis*cover, *dis*believe, *di*vide.

Ex, e, ec, or ef —*out*, or *out of*; as, *ex*tend, *ex*clude.

Em, or en —*in, into*, or *on*; as, *em*bark, *en*throne.

Extra —*beyond*; as, *extra*ordinary.

In, or ig, il, im, and ir —*in, into, upon*, or *not*; as, *in*case, *in*sert, *im*pose, *il*legal.

Inter —*between* or *among*; as, *inter*mix.

Intro —*among*; as, *intro*duce.

Mis —*wrong, defect, error*; as, *mis*conduct, *mis*call.

Ob, or oc, of, and op —*in the way, against, out*; as, *ob*struct, *op*pose.

Per —*through*, or *thoroughly*; as, *per*vade, *per*fect.

Post —*after*; as, *post*script.

Pre —*before*; as, *pre*fix, *pre*dict.

Preter —*beyond*; as, *preter*natural.

Pro —*for, forward*, or *forth*; as, *pro*noun, *pro*ceed, *pro*duce.

Re —*back, again*, or *anew*; as, *re*call, *re*build, *re*new.

Se —*aside, apart*, or *without*; as, *se*cede, *se*clude.

Sub, or suc, suf, sug, sup, and sus —*under*; as, *sub*ject, *sug*gest, *sup*port.

Syn, or sy, syl, and sym —*together, with*; as, *syn*agogue, *sym*pathy.

Super, or sur —*above, over, more than enough*; as, *super*add, *super*fluous, *sur*pass.

Trans —*over, beyond, across*; as, *trans*gress, *trans*atlantic.

Un —with verbs, *to undo*; as, *un*furl, *un*seal.—with adjectives and adverbs, it signifies *not*; as, *un*kind, *un*justly.

.With —*from* or *against*; as, *with*draw, *with*stand.

OF SUFFIXES.

The following denote the person who is in a certain state or condition, or who does a certain thing.

An, or ian —Histori*an*, Christi*an*.

Ant —disput*ant*, inhabit*ant*.

Ar —liar, begga*r*.
Ard —drunk*ard*, slugga*rd*.
Ary —antigua*ry*, adversa*ry*.
Ate —magist*rate*, associ*ate*.
Ee —trust*ee*, patent*ee*.
Eer.—engin*eer*, auction*eer*.
Ent —stud*ent*, ag*ent*.
Er —bak*er*, philosoph*er*.
Ist —art*ist*, botan*ist*.
Ite —favor*ite*, hypo*crite*.
Ive —rela*tive*, cap*tive*.
Or —execu*tor*, doc*tor*.
Ster —song*ster*, team*ster*.
Ling —*little, young; as, stripling, darling*.

The following relate to things.

Acy —*state or condition;* as, obstin*acy*, celib*acy*.
Age —*condition, compensation;* as, bond*age*, dot*age*, post*age*.
Al —*doing a thing;* as, denial, removal.
Ance, ancy —*state of being;* as, ignor*ance*, vigil*ance*, con*stancy*.
Ary —*place in which;* as, semin*ary*, libr*ary*.
Cle and cule —*little;* as, canti*cle*, glob*ule*.
Dom —*state or condition, extent of rule;* as, free*dom*, king*dom*.
Ence, ency —*state of being;* as, dilig*ence*, emerg*ency*.
Escence —*growing, becoming;* as, convale*scence*, efferve*scence*.
Hood —*condition;* as, boy*hood*.
Ics —*science of;* as, mathemat*ics*, polit*ics*.
Ion —*doing a thing, state of being;* as, creat*ion*, rebell*ion*.
Ism —*condition, doctrine;* as, barbar*ism*, stoic*ism*.
Ment —*state of being, thing done;* as, abase*ment*, abridg*ment*.
Mony —*state of being, thing done;* as, har*mony*, testi*mony*.
Ness —*state of being, or quality;* as, blessed*ness*, soft*ness*.
Ory —*place in which;* as, fact*ory*, arm*ory*.
Ship —*state, office;* as, partner*ship*, clerk*ship*.
Tude —*condition;* as, disquie*tude*, servi*tude*.
Ty —*state of;* as, fertili*ty*, abili*ty*.
Ure —*the thing, state, or act;* as, ves*ture*, compos*ure*, de*parture*.

SUFFIXES

USED TO FORM ADJECTIVES.

The following denote belonging, relating, or pertaining to.

Ac, ic, ical —demoniac, despotic, political.
Al —filial, annual, ethereal.
An —American, republican.
Ar —insular, ocular.
Ary —planetary, literary.
Ine —marine, feminine.

The following denote being or having.

Ant —abundant, brilliant.
Ate —accurate, temperate.
Ent —absent, benevolent.
Ous —dangerous, populous.

The following are of various significations.

Ble —*may or can be, worthy of;* as, arable laudable, audible.
En —*made of;* as, wooden.
Ful —*full of;* as, joyful, careful.
Ile —*may or can be, quality;* as, ductile, docile.
Ish —*resembling, little of;* as, boyish, greenish.
Ive —*having power, tending to produce;* as, decisive, destructive.
Less —*not having;* as, cloudless, fearless.
Like, ly —*resembling;* as, warlike, friendly.
Ory —*pertaining to, giving;* as, prefatory, admonitory.
Some —*full of;* as troublesome.
y —*full of, made of;* as, wealthy, horny.

SUFFIXES

USED TO FORM VERBS, THE GENERAL SIGNIFICATION OF WHICH IS, TO MAKE, GIVE, DO, OR SUFFER.

Ate —renovate, operate.
En —harden, darken.

Fy —puri*fy*, forti*fy*.
Ish —publi*sh*, dimini*sh*.
Ise, ize —chasti*se*, agoni*ze*.

SUFFIXES

USED TO FORM ADVERBS.

Ly —*like, manner or way ;* as, bold*ly*, wise*ly*.
Ward —*direction of ;* as, for*ward*, east*ward*.

Some of the foregoing suffixes have additional meanings, which it would require remarks of considerable length to unfold, and which can best be learned by reference to a dictionary and by practice.

CARDINAL NUMBERS.

Figures.	Letters.	Names.	Figures.	Letters.	Names.
1	I	one	21	XXI	twenty-one
2	II	two	22	XXII	twenty-two
3	III	three	23	XXIII	twenty-three
4	IV	four	30	XXX	thirty
5	V	five	40	XL	forty
6	VI	six	50	L	fifty
7	VII	seven	60	LX	sixty
8	VIII	eight	70	LXX	seventy
9	IX	nine	80	LXXX	eighty
10	X	ten	90	XC	ninety
11	XI	eleven	100	C	one hundred
12	XII	twelve	200	CC	two hundred
13	XIII	thirteen	300	CCC	three hundred
14	XIV	fourteen	400	CCCC	four hundred
15	XV	fifteen	500	D	five hundred
16	XVI	sixteen	600	DC	six hundred
17	XVII	seventeen	700	DCC	seven hundred
18	XVIII	eighteen	800	DCCC	eight hundred
19	XIX	nineteen	900	DCCCC	nine hundred
20	XX	twenty	1000	M	one thousand

1840   MDCCCXL   one thousand eight hundred and forty.

ORDINAL NUMBERS.

1st	first	21st	twenty-first
2nd	second	22nd	twenty-second
3rd	third	23rd	twenty-third
4th	fourth	24th &c.	twenty-fourth
5th &c.	fifth	30th	thirtieth
10th	tenth	40th	fortieth
11th	eleventh	50th &c.	fiftieth
12th	twelfth	100th	one hundreth
13th &c.	thirteenth	200th &c.	two hundreth
20th	twentieth	1000th	one thousandth
		2000th &c.	two thousandth.

ABBREVIATIONS.

A. or Ans. Answer.
A. A. S. Fellow of the American Academy.
A. B. Batchelor of Arts.
Acct. Account.
A. D. In the year of our Lord.
Al. Alabama.
A. M. { Master of Arts. Before noon. In the year of the world.
Apr. April.
Att'y. Attorney.
Aug. August.
Ark. Arkansas.
B. V. Blessed Virgin.
C. or cent. a hundred.
C. A. S. Fellow of the Connecticut Academy.
Cant. Canticles.
Capt. Captain.
Chap. Chapter.
Chron. Chronicles.
Co. Company, or County.
Col. Colonel.
Com. Commissioner. Commodore.
Conn. or Ct. Connecticut.
Const. Constable.
Cor. Corinthians.
Cr. Credit. Creditor.

Cts. Cents.
Cwt. Hundred weight.
D. C. District of Columbia.
D. D. Doctor of Divinity.
Dea. Deacon.
Dec. December.
Del. Delaware.
Dept. Deputy.
Deut. Deuteronomy.
Do. or Ditto. The same.
Dr. Doctor, or Debtor.
E. East.
Eccl. Ecclesiastes.
Ed. Editor, or Edition.
E. G. For example.
Eng. England, or English.
Ep. Epistle.
Eph. Ephesians.
Esa. Esaias.
Esq. Esquire.
Etc. and so forth.
Ex. Example, or Exodus.
Exr. Executor.
Feb. February.
Fig. Figure.
Fr. France, or Francis.
Flor. Florida.
F. R. S. Fellow of the Royal Society.
Gal. Galatians.

Gen. Genesis, or General.
Gent. Gentleman.
Ga. Georgia.
Gov. Governor.
Heb. Hebrews.
Hhd. Hogshead.
Hon. Honorable.
Hund. Hundred.
Ibid. In the same place.
Id. The same.
i. e. That is.
Ind. or Ia. Indiana.
Inst. Instant.
Ill. Illinois.
Ja. James.
Jac. Jacob.
Jan January.
Jno. John.
Jos. Joseph.
Josh. Joshua.
Jun. Junior.
Km. Kingdom.
Ky. Kentucky.
Lam. Lamentations.
Lat. Latitude.
lbs. Pounds.
L. C. Lower Canada.
Lev. Leviticus.
Lieut. Lieutenant.
LL D. Doctor of Laws.
Lon. Longitude.
Lou. or La. Louisiana.
L. S. Place of the Seal.
Maj. Major.
Mi. Mississippi.
Mass. Massachusetts.
Mich. Michigan.
Mo. Missouri.
M. C. Member of Congress.
M. D. Doctor of Physic.
Md. Maryland.
Me. Maine.
Mr. Master, or Mister.
Mrs. Mistress.
Messrs. Gentlemen, or Sirs.
MS. Manuscript.
MSS. Manuscripts.
N. North.
N. B. Note well.
N. C. North Carolina.
N. H. New Hampshire.
N. J. New Jersey.

No. Number.
Nov. November.
N. S. New Style.
N. W. T. North Western Territory.
N. Y. New York.
O. Ohio.
Obj. Objection.
Obt. Obedient.
Oct. October.
O. S. Old Style.
Parl. Parliament.
Penn. or Pa. Pennsylvania.
Per. By the ; as per cent., by the hundred.
Pet. Peter.
Phil. Philippians, or Philip.
Philom. A lover of learning.
P. M. Post Master, or afternoon.
P. O. Post Office.
Pres. President.
Prof. Professor.
P. S. Postscript.
Ps. Psalm.
Q. Question.
q. d. As if he should say.
q. l. As much as you please.
q. s. A sufficient quantity.
Regr. Register.
Rep. Representative.
Rev. Revelation, or Reverend
Rt. Hon. Right Honorable.
R. I. Rhode Island.
Rom. Romans.
S. South.
S. C. South Carolina.
Sec. Secretary.
Sect. Section.
Sen. Senator, or Senior.
Sept. September.
Serg. Sergeant.
Servt. Servant.
St. Saint.
S. T. D. Doctor of Divinity.
S. T. P. Professor of Divinity.
ss. To wit ; namely.
Tenn. or Te. Tennessee.
Thess. Thessalonians.
Tho. Thomas.
Tim. Timothy.
U. C. Upper Canada.
Ult. The last.
U. S. A. United States of America.

V. or Vide ; See.	Wm. William.
Va. Virginia.	Wp. Worship.
Viz. To wit ; namely.	Wt. Weight.
Vt. Vermont.	Yd. Yard.
W. West.	&. And.
W. I. West Indies.	&c. And so forth.

POINTS, MARKS, AND CAPITAL LETTERS.

A comma,	,	A caret,	^
A semicolon,	;	A quotation,	" "
A colon,	:	A section,	§
A period,	.	An index,	☞
An interrogation point,	?	A paragraph,	¶
An exclamation point,	!	Brackets,	[ ]
A hyphen,	-	A dash,	—
A parenthesis,	( )	A brace,	{
An apostrophe,	'		
A diæresis,		..	

A comma denotes that the voice must stop as long as in pronouncing one syllable.

A semicolon denotes a pause twice as long as a comma.

A colon denotes a pause three times as long as a comma.

A period denotes a pause four times as long as a comma.

An interrogation point shows that a question is asked.

An exclamation point is a mark of wonder, or some other strong emotion.

A hyphen connects compound words, as honey-comb.

A parenthesis includes something affecting the sense, but which might be omitted without material injury.

An apostrophe shows the omission of one or more letters, as giv'n, tho', for though, given.

It also denotes the possessive case, as Robert's pen.

A caret shows that a letter, word, or figure, in writing, has
been omitted through mistake, as mo_row.

A quotation shows that what is between the marks, is in the words of some other author.

A section divides a chapter, or discourse into parts.

An index points to what requires particular attention.

A paragraph shows the beginning of a new topic.

Brackets include something explanatory.

A dash shows a pause, sometimes abrupt; or a change of subject.

A brace connects several words or lines.

A diœresis shows that the vowel over which it stands is sounded by itself, as creätion.

An asterisk or star, a dagger, and other marks, with letters and figures, refer to the margin or bottom of the page; as, * † ‡ §.

Capital letters should be used, at the beginning of every book, chapter, and sentence; at the beginning of all the names of God; of proper names of persons, places, rivers, mountains, seas, lakes, ships, &c.; and of all adjectives derived from proper names; at the beginning of a quotation, and of lines of poetry, and, sometimes, of an important word in a sentence.

I and O are always written in capitals.

RULES FOR SPELLING.

I. Words of one syllable, and words of more than one syllable accented on the last, ending in a single consonant after a single vowel, double that consonant, when another syllable beginning with a vowel is added; as, sun, sunny; blot, blotting, blotted; permit, permitting, permitted; begin, beginner.

Words ending in *x* do not follow this rule, as wax, waxing; nor those in which the additional syllable changes the accent, as confer, conference. To this, *excellence* is an exception.

II. But if the last consonant is not preceded by a single vowel, or the accent is not on the last syllable, the consonant is *not* doubled; as, toil, toiling; read, reader; suffer, suffering, sufferer.

In regard to most of the verbs ending in *l*, that come under this rule, and also the derivatives of the word *worship*, there is still a difference of usage. Some, for example, write travel, traveling, traveler—worship, worshiping, worshiper; and others, travelling, traveller—worshipping,

III. Words ending in two or more consonants, do not double the last letter, when another syllable is added; as, mend, mending; watch, watching, watcher; expect, expecting, expected.

IV. Monosyllables ending in *f, l*, or *s*, have these consonants double, when preceded by a single vowel; as, staff, hill, glass.

If, of, as, is, has, his, was, gas, yes, this, us, and *thus*, are exceptions.

V. Monosyllables, ending in any consonant but *f, l*, or *s*, do not have the final consonant double, excepting *add, jagg, ebb, egg, inn, odd, butt, err, buzz*; to which some add *bunn*, and *purr*.

VI. When an addition is made to a word ending in y, preceded by a *consonant*, the *y* is changed into *i*; as, cry, cries; try, triest, trieth; happy, happier, happiest, happiness; pity, pitied, pitiable, pitiful; duty, duties.

But before *ing* the *y* is retained; as, pity, pitying; carry, carrying.

VII. When an addition is made to a word ending in y, preceded by a *vowel*, the *y* is not changed; as, day, days; key, keys; boy, boys; valley, valleys; money, moneys; decay, decaying, decayed; convey, conveying, conveyed; employ, employer.

Laid, paid, said, and *saith*, from lay, pay, and say, are exceptions.

VIII. Words ending in double consonants retain both, when an additional termination is made; as, careless, carelessness; success, successful.

Some except from this rule *dulness, fulness, skilful*, and *wilful*.

IX. When a vowel, or a termination beginning with a vowel, is added to a word ending in silent *e*, the *e* is generally omitted; as, shine, shiny; save, saving; force, forced, forcible.

The *e* is retained in *hoeing* and *shoeing*, and in such adjectives ending in *able* as are derived from words that end in *ce, ge*, or *ee*; as, peaceable, traceable, changeable, chargeable, serviceable, manageable, marriageable, agreeable.

X. If the added termination is a consonant, or begins with a consonant, the silent *e* is generally retained; as, fate, fates; hate, hateful; pale, paleness.

Judgment, lodgment, abridgment, argument, acknowledgment, duly, truly, awful, wholly, are exceptions.

XI. In forming the present participle of verbs ending in *ie,* the *e* is dropped, and the *i* changed into *y;* as, lie, lying. But in the other variations of such verbs, the *i* and the *e* are retained; as lie, liest, lieth or lies, lied.

The other verbs in *ie,* are hie, die, tie, vie, and their compounds.

XII. The plural of nouns is generally formed by adding *s* to the singular; as, book, books; dove, doves; monarch, monarchs.

When the singular ends in *x, ss, sh,* and *ch* as in porch, the plural is formed by adding *es;* as, tax, taxes; class, classes; fish, fishes; porch, porches.

When the singular ends in *f* or *fe,* the plural is sometimes formed by changing these terminations into *ves;* as, half, halves; life, lives.

XIII. The past tense and past participle of regular verbs, are formed by the addition of *ed,* and the present participle by that of *ing;* as, plant, planted, planting. Silent *e* at the end is dropped; as, love, loved, loving.

When *ed,* in this case, follows *t* or *d,* it is pronounced as an additional syllable; as, part, part-ed; end, end-ed.

When it follows any other letter, the *e* is usually silent, and the *d* is united in pronunciation with the preceding syllable; as, curb, curb'd; love, lov'd; tame, tam'd; and its sound is sometimes changed into that of *t;* as, pluck, pluck'd,—pronounced *pluckt.*

XIV. The correct spelling of words in common use, excepting proper names, containing the diphthong *ei* or *ie,* may be determined thus:

It is *ei,* when the diphthong has any of the sounds of *a;* as in deign, their:—when it is followed immediately by *t,* or the sound of *t;* as in either, receipt, height:—when, with the preceding letter, it has the sound of *see;* as in deceit, receive, ceil, seize, excepting *siege, glacier, financier,* and *cuirassier.*

It is also *ei* in *eider, foreign, sovereign, heifer, inveigle, leisure, obeisance, plebeian, teil, weird,* and *non-pareil.*

In all other cases it is *ie.*

XV. Compound words generally retain the spelling of the simple words which compose them; as, workman; herein.

Many words ending with double *l,* and some others, are ; as, already, welfare, wherever.

ADDITIONAL REMARKS TO TEACHERS.

In those lessons which consist of words classed in reference to the *general resemblance* of the obscure sounds in the closing, unaccented syllables, it is not intended that these syllables have always the *same sound*. The teacher will be careful to notice this; as in Lessons 100, 101, 143, 154, 155, and others of a similar kind.

In addition to those modes of using the lessons which have been already mentioned in the *Directions to Teachers*, there are some others that may be pursued to advantage. Thus in Lesson 90, let the teacher ask for a word ending in *are* with the sound of *a* as in bare; then for another ending with the same sound, but spelt differently; then, for another; and so on. The same course may be pursued in Lessons of a similar construction.

In many lessons, after announcing a word, the selection being made from the various columns indiscriminately, the scholars, especially those who are somewhat advanced, may be required to answer by repeating only that part of the word which contains a peculiar difficulty. Thus in Lesson 76, the teacher can say "veto," and the scholar will reply, *o;*—"cocoa," and the answer will be, *o a;*—"blow, and the answer will be, *o w;*—"dough," "beau," "owe," and "hoe;" and the answers will be, *o u g h, e a u, o w e,* and *o e.* In Lesson 135, the teacher can say "vacant," and the scholar will reply, *a n t;*—"decent," "tyrant," "moment," and the answers will successively be, *e n t,—a n t,* and *e n t.*

In Lessons containing words in which silent letters are found, it will be a profitable exercise to call upon the scholars to repeat them, or to write them on the blackboard, from memory.

In giving out words to be spelt by the lower classes, the teacher may occasionally pronounce the vowel sounds in the unaccented syllables fully and distinctly; but generally the words should be pronounced, both by teacher and scholar, as in common conversation and good speaking.

INDEX.

This Index is designed for the more advanced scholars, and especially for teachers, and those who wish to attend, with critical accuracy, to the anomalies of orthography and pronunciation. It will enable the teacher to form a methodical view and analysis of many of these anomalies. He can use the lessons which contain them in reviewing; in testing the accuracy of the learner; in aiding him to overcome his peculiar difficulties; and in such other practical exercises as may be deemed expedient.

PART I.

Vowel sounds, found in monosyllables, and sometimes in the closing syllables, but oftener in the preceding.

Sound of o, as in move.	*Sound of o and ow, as in bound.*

PART II.

Long vowel sounds, found in monosyllables, and in the closing syllables.

PART III.

The consonants and their sounds, found usually in monosyllables, and in the closing syllables.

The Index may be used by those who are at a loss with regard to the orthography of certain words, or classes of words, by referring to the Lessons in which they are to be found, and thus the recollection of them be promoted by cultivating a methodical memory. For example, one may not know how to spell the word *laugh.* His ear, however, readily notices the vowel sound of *a as in bar* which it contains. He finds this sound in Part I. and is referred to Lessons 17 and 99, in one of which the word will be found.

The word *portmanteau* ends with the long sound of *o.* This is found in Part II. and reference is made to Lesson 76, which contains that word.

The word *confidence* ends with the sound of *s.* This will be found in Part III. together with the two terminating syllables which constitute the perplexity, *ance* and *ence.* Reference is made to Lessons 157 and 158 in one of which the word will be found.

A little practice will make this use of the Index easy.

THE END.

THE FOLLOWING VALUABLE BOOKS

ARE PUBLISHED BY

WILLIAM J. HAMERSLEY,

HARTFORD, CONN.

AND CAN BE OBTAINED OF PHILLIPS, SAMPSON & CO., W. J. REYNOLDS & CO., R. S. DAVIS & CO., &C., &C., BOSTON; IVISON & PHINNEY, D APPLETON & CO., CLARK, AUSTIN, & SMITH, D. BURGESS & CO., A. S. BARNES & CO., &C., &C., NEW YORK; J. B. LIPPINCOTT & CO., H. COWPERTHWAIT & CO., E H. BUTLER & CO., &C., &C., PHILADELPHIA.

And of the Booksellers generally.

School and College Series.

WOODBRIDGE AND WILLARD'S UNIVERSAL GEOGRAPHY.—Accompanied by an Atlas, Physical and Political. This is the only Geography suitable for High Schools. It is adopted in many of the principal seminaries in the Union. The work has been translated into the German language, and is used as a text-book in some of the first schools in Germany.

WILLARD'S ANCIENT GEOGRAPHY AND ATLAS.—This work has been recently revised by the author, with the assistance of Mr. WALTER, Professor of Geography in the Royal Schools of Berlin, Prussia.

WOODBRIDGE'S MODERN SCHOOL GEOGRAPHY.—Accompanied by an Atlas, Physical and Political. The attention of school committees and others is particularly invited to this work. Wherever introduced, it has given great satisfaction. It is confidently claimed to be the best School Geography before the public. It is recommended in the highest terms by Rev. T. H. Gallaudet; Rt. Rev. Thomas C. Brownell; Prof. Goodrich, of Yale College; Rev. Dr. Bushnell; Wm. A. Alcott, Esq.; Bishop Potter, of Pennsylvania; Rev. Simson North, President of Hamilton College; Emerson Davis, Esq., of Massachusetts; and by numerous practical teachers and other friends of education.

FLINT'S SURVEYING.—With new rules for the deviations of the Compass. Revised Edition.

ROBBINS' OUTLINES OF HISTORY.—New Edition, enlarged and improved. This work has lately received important additions, making it now a *complete* text-book of History.

THE PRACTICAL SPELLING-BOOK.—By T. H. Gallaudet and H. Hooker—on a new plan.

The attention of teachers is respectfully invited to an examination of the peculiar features of this work.

FIRST LESSONS ON NATURAL PHILOSOPHY.—*Parts 1 and 2.*—By Mary A. Swift.—These Books, for clearness of explanation and illustration, are unequaled by any other work on the subject, for young children. They are used in every State in the Union.

Greek Series.

The following series of Greek text-books have been received with un-qualified favor by classical teachers. Sophocles' Greek Grammar is used in Harvard, Yale, and many other of the principal colleges in the Union, and in a large number of High Schools and Academies.

SOPHOCLES' Greek Lessons.
"   First Book in Greek.
"   Greek Grammar, old edition.
"   Greek Grammar, revised edition.
"   Romaic Grammar.
"   Greek Exercises.
"   "   Exercises and Key.
"   "   Verbs.
Felton's Greek Reader.
Crusius' Homeric Lexicon.

THE COLUMBIAN DRAWING BOOK.—Containing 36 plain and tinted plates. Folio. Embracing a progressive series of studies, adapted from the first masters, by C. Kuchel. With instructions, by Gervase Wheeler—The Drawings by D'Avignon, Kuchel, and others. This is the most elegant Drawing Book published in the country.

JOHNSON'S PHILOSOPHICAL CHARTS—designed for the use of Schools and Academies, to illustrate the different branches of Natural Philosophy. The figures are contained on 10 large mounted Charts (33 × 48), and are designed to be used either with or without a text-book. They answer well to accompany lectures and take the place in a great measure, of apparatus. When not in use by the class, they can be hung around the school-room, thus rendering familiar many parts of the Science, even to those who have not paid especial attention to it. The Charts are accompanied by a Key explaining the figures, &c.

THE CLASS BOOK OF NATURE.—Containing Lessons on the Universe, the Three Kingdoms of Nature, and the Form and Structure of the Human Body. With Questions, and numerous Engravings. Highly recommended, and extensively used.

THE PROGRESSIVE DRAWING STUDIES—being a series of five numbers, each containing four Studies, Folio; executed in the highest style of the art. The designs are of general selection, embracing Landscapes, Buildings, Animals, the Human Figure, Heads, &c., &c. The series, the publisher is confident is not excelled by anything of the kind in the market, and requests for it the attention of Drawing Teachers, Students, Amateurs, and others.

THE BOOK OF NATURE.—By John Mason Good, M. D., F. R. S., F. R. S. L. &c., &c., from the last London Edition to which is now prefixed a sketch of the Author's Life. Complete in one volume.

CONVERSATION ON CHEMISTRY—by J. V. Blake, adapted from the English edition—and designed as a text-book for that Science.